Joint Venture

A Backstage Rock and Roll Journey

Ed Kleinman

Order this book online at www.trafford.com
or email orders@trafford.com

Most Trafford titles are also available at major online book retailers.

Printed in the United States of America.

ISBN: 978-1-4669-9775-2 (sc)
ISBN: 978-1-4669-9774-5 (hc)
ISBN: 978-1-4669-9776-9 (e)

Library of Congress Control Number: 2013910779

Trafford rev. 06/28/2013

 www.trafford.com

North America & international
toll-free: 1 888 232 4444 (USA & Canada)
fax: 812 355 4082

I dedicate this book to my wife, Susan, who has worked alongside me and who has stood by me and kept me out of trouble.

Also to my son, Michael, whom I wish to teach that, with desire, commitment, and the understanding that you are always learning, you can be successful at whatever you choose to do, not only at work, but also at play. Smile, stay positive, and do your best always. Always remember to take responsibility for your actions, treat everyone with respect, and help all those you can.

And finally, to all you rockers out there, whether you are in the music industry or any type of business, remember:

THE SHOW MUST GO ON!
PERFORM AT YOUR MAXIMUM BEST!

ACKNOWLEDGMENTS

First, thank you Susan Erlichman, my wife, for helping me through the years.

I'd also like to thank Don Johnson, wherever he may be. Reading my story, if it doesn't become apparent that rolling joints for him and Danny got me started in the world of rock and roll, well, put your joint down now. You've already smoked too much.

Thanks to Barry Platnick, my entertainment lawyer, for writing good contracts for my management company; Bill Zysblat, my accountant, who kept me from going broke; and Marty Sinclair, for backing our management company and believing that we could make it happen.

In addition, I would like to thank all the bands, musicians, and coworkers I've worked with over the years, especially members of The Blues Project and Blood, Sweat & Tears. And John Finley, of Rhinoceros, for the great picture of that group. Glad you're still performing. Also to Gary Van Scyoc for his help with Pig Iron and Elephant's Memory information and pictures. Also Puggy DeRosa and his band Everyone, LeBlanc & Carr, The Stranglers, John Cale, Jerome "Bigfoot" Brailey, Genya Ravan for her great picture, and my former coworker Larry Waterman for teaching me things on and off the road that helped me get better at my job. And to Ava Rave, for her great pictures from The Stranglers' 1980 tour, when we all looked like kids.

Thank you to Lee Boot, who urged me to write my memoir and relate some of it to the business I'm in now. A good friend and a great artist, Lee also created this book's cover art. And to Rush Burkhardt, a friend and colleague who first prodded me quite a few years ago to write this book with, "Put it in writing before you forget," and to Bob Ortiz for his great advice on how to get started. Special thanks also go to Jim Sasena for help with the book title.

More special thanks to Dianne McCann for her expert help with my final editing.

Also, thank you, May Pang, for giving me insight into getting this book published. And not only for some great photos to use, but also for having her act together during the John and Yoko and Elephant's Memory days. Thanks for still being a good friend.

IF I LEFT SOMEONE OUT, MY APOLOGIES TO YOU AND MUCH THANKS. WITHOUT YOU, THIS WOULD NOT HAVE BEEN POSSIBLE.

PROLOGUE . . . the beginning

One tells a story of days gone by. A flash of your history, a snapshot of an instant. Be it a minute, an hour, a day, or a year, it matters none. Something jogs your brain cells where past history is stored. You smile, and you think you have something worth telling.

My story is about my 18 years in the music industry, from 1966 to 1984 . . . from starting as a part-time roadie making just enough money to buy cigarettes and put gas into my car . . . to being able to hang out with musicians and tell lovely young ladies, "I'm with the band. Ya wanna meet one of 'em?" . . . to forming my own entertainment management company . . . until eventually leaving the business world of rock and roll.

Those years, especially my early years, brought a great deal of change to the music world and to all corners of society. It was the 1960s, the youth movement was stirring, and we all felt it. As young people, we felt freer than our parents ever had, so we took advantage of it. And the music played on. We fought for equality for all, we protested the Vietnam War, and we marched. The music got stronger, too—more political, more active in supporting change. No wonder the Grateful Dead came to sing, "What a long, strange trip it's been."

Lucky for me, I was there for all of it. In fact, I was often on the inside, looking out—but not from the stage. I worked behind the music scenes, playing my part to make it happen.

What I never did was ask for autographs. That was a very big NO if you were working with any bands or even simply hanging out with the musicians or artists. The other thing I didn't do during those years—but probably should have—was keep a journal.

Still, since that time, in these past 20 years, what I learned working in the music industry has helped me further my career in my sales force development role. I'd also like to think that I'm still learning, still rockin', still helping others. What the future brings, we shall see. Where the present generation goes remains to be seen. I hope it's good, good for all, good for the world.

So where do I begin?

A few years ago, over shots of tequila, my friends Lee Boot and Rush Burkhardt urged me to put my memories, my experiences down on paper before I grew too old to even remember who I am. So I started a journal on December 26, 2006, in Cuernavaca, Mexico.

Here, in these pages, I relive my rock and roll journey, recalled as best I can. This is the way I saw it, and now I invite you to come along.

THE REAL BEGINNING . . . more minutes, more hours, more days, more years

To go forward, I have to go back quite a way, back in time when I got interested in what was being played on the radio in the mid-1950s. I was an Elvis Presley fan at age 10. I loved his early Sun Sessions recordings and his performances on *The Ed Sullivan Show*. I even had a mop handle with a rope on it, making believe it was a guitar, and I'd wiggle and strum to Elvis' music along with that of other rock and rollers.

Having a brother six years older was a plus. He had a DA haircut, motorcycle boots, jeans, and souped-up cars. From the Marlon Brando *Wild Ones* to the James Dean *Rebels without a Cause* types, rock and rollers were the focal point of a lot of people who hated this early music and thought it was ruining kids everywhere. Were they in for the surprise coming at them by the 1960s.

I got to listen to a lot of the music my brother and his friends were listening and dancing to, from the doo-woppers to the real R&B/blues artists along with the up-and-coming rock and roll bands. Through him, I also found the legendary disc jockey, Alan Freed. His Cleveland radio show was broadcasted on a NYC station, which I listened to in my hometown of Jersey City, NJ, where I was born and raised.

My friends and I came from working-class families, living in a racially mixed neighborhood of six-family tenement houses and two-family homes. No lawns, just sidewalks and streets to play in. But we had music. Real music to grasp on to. Music that meant something to us, to sing in alleys, hallways, and bathrooms; to hum in class; and to inspire us to start collecting 45 rpms. I remember my first 45, "Why Do Fools Fall in Love" by Frankie Lymon and the Teenagers.

We had our own music, so to speak. No more of what our parents listened to. We were on the go. It was ours, and we were not going to let anyone take that away. We had Elvis for a while and Little Richard, Bill Haley and the Comets, Buddy Holly, Gene Vincent and Eddie Cochran. And blues singers such as Muddy Waters, Bo Diddley, B.B. King, and more. Radio was getting more adventurous. Sure some stations were so-called "Negro radio stations," but we didn't care. We wanted more, and we found it. Top 40 was not all we had. Thank you, Mr. Freed and others.

My mother began to push me to take piano lessons, even guitar lessons. She would say, "You like music so much, learn to play something."

For some reason, I had no interest or desire to learn. Maybe it was a protest against my mom for trying to push me. Who knows? It was too many years ago. But I liked the music. I learned to dance early on while in day camp and could lindy as well as anyone on *American Bandstand*. It did help with girlfriends at high school dances and various dances at community centers, etc. No problem.

EXPLORATION . . . more music and off to Greenwich Village

I was now in high school. Wearing a torn sweatshirt, I read all of Jack Kerouac's books and I acted like what I knew about the Beat Generation. I read beat poets, got into more jazz and now folk music, but not just the Kingston Trio. I listened to early Bob Dylan, Joan Baez, and varied others. And I joined a folk music club at the local Jewish Community Center (JCC) and heard blues, folk, more jazz, and even listened to the likes of Howlin' Wolf and Jimmy Reed on a wire recorder. The world was opening up for me.

One evening after the music club had ended, I was sitting at the snack bar when in walked a couple of guys around my age. I never saw them before, but one was carrying a jazz album by Ahmad Jamal, which I had also owned. (In fact, it was my only jazz album.) For some reason, they looked over at me, and I asked if they had listened to the album. They said no, but they were on the way to do so. I told them I had the album, too, and it was great. I really liked piano jazz. They asked if I wanted to join them. Who could pass up that invite?

So, off I went, into what became a very close friendship, a new experience with a cross section of new people. The first two were Nicky Walton and Howie Dimont. To this day, I still occasionally contact Howie. As for Nicky, more to come regarding him.

From these relationships came the exploration of Greenwich Village. Kerouac's books turned me on to the name Greenwich Village. Nicky and Howie turned me on to the real place. My own feet on the ground in the Village! They had been there often. Going to coffee houses to hear music, drink coffee, and hang out. I couldn't have asked for anything better. Off I went.

I had to be home by midnight, however, or my mom was going to yell and scream (Jewish mom). I was 14 going on 15. So, given we had in Jersey City a subway that went into NYC with, by chance, a stop at 9th Street and 6th Avenue in Greenwich Village, what more could a young kid want especially given what I thought I knew about this place. I had easy access and two new friends who had at least been there before. As long as I was home by midnight, all was cool.

We explored Washington Square Park and listened to the folkies. This was 1960 to 1962. The Playhouse Café on McDougal Street, named after the Playhouse Theater next door, became our hangout. I met so many wonderful new friends there. I also found out that we were not the only teenagers trying to discover a new world, a new freedom, all which seemed to revolve around music, art, and theater.

Musicians would come in to play a few songs, then pass the hat for change, dollars, and phone numbers, whatever. They would make the rounds of other coffee houses in the area as well. Poets came and read their latest, too.

I remember Peter, Paul, and Mary playing there a few times prior to becoming well known. Also, I remember hearing folkie Dave Van Ronk, readings by poet Allen Ginsberg, and seeing drawings by an artist named Margaret Keane, whose paintings of people all had these wonderful, big eyes.

I wish I could remember more and remember the names of some of the people I hung out with. They helped me grow up even more. Most were New Yorkers; a few were from South America, but now lived in New York. We were all around the same age, give or take a year or two. We had a place to meet, talk, and grow. Thank you, dear past friends. You helped me on a journey to experience new things and new people and to understand that we all shared a similar world vision. Looking back, growing up in Jersey City, so close to NYC, was incredible. I wish I had kept a journal.

With my Jersey City friends and New York friends, I began to experience a lot of new music, new places to see, new people to know, and new insight that the world was changing and people had something to say about it. There were real discussions and dialogues regarding what we thought about things. We were learning about who we were and maybe learning some things that helped who we would become in later years. This was all new to me and I soaked it up, grateful that I, too, at 15 was accepted for my thoughts and opinions. This went on for a few years and, by the time high school was ending, I had to decide what was next.

I was a senior when a friend, Lanny, asked if I wanted to go to Carnegie Hall on New Year's Eve to hear some live jazz. How could I pass that up? Times Square, New Year's Eve, and live jazz from the likes of Nina Simone, John Coltrane, Thelonious Monk, Charlie Parker, and Sonny Rollins—WHEW, what a way to end the year. What a way to get turned on to even more jazz, and LIVE! We sat in the very last row in the nosebleed section. It was a memorable time and my first time to celebrate New Year's Eve in Times Square.

NICKY. We became close friends; he had an older brother named Mike. We were both high school sophomores when we met, in different high schools. We liked the same music, a lot of the same people, and we hung out at the JCC in Jersey City. I had to take a bus from my neighborhood to get to the JCC, and Nicky lived right down the street from there. Given he lived down the block, we also hung out at his house, or at least on his front porch. His mom was great and was able to keep most of us under control.

I met a lot of people through Nicky, "the good, the bad, and the ugly" as I came to name them. Some older, some high school dropouts, some Jews, some not. For the most part, we all went to the same parties, or crashed a lot of them. At one point, I would be invited and told not to bring anyone except Nicky. So the two of us would go off to the parties, and, at other times, we were off to the Village. Maybe we were late beatniks, or early hippies before that era arrived.

I write about Nicky because of his influence on me growing up, on the music we shared. Nicky got into trouble in our senior year. He was accused of the statutory rape of a minor. Not sure it was true. We all knew the girl. She was the sister of one of the guys who hung out with us. She had a crush on Nicky, but he didn't return the feelings. From there, only she knows.

Nicky was sent away to finish high school in Maine. We always stayed in touch when he came home to visit. Upon graduation, he enlisted in the army. It was 1964 or 1965, and the Vietnam War was beginning to get more active. He came home from boot camp and had received his orders to ship out to Vietnam.

Nicky was far from a war supporter. The army was a way out for him, I guess.

The way I got the story, he and a cousin of his were drinking heavily. His cousin went off to the store to get more alcohol, and when he returned, Nicky was on the floor, bleeding from a gunshot. Did he try to commit suicide? Was he trying to wound himself to get out of going to Vietnam?

There was even a rumor that his cousin had shot him. I never believed that, and a few years later, I became friendly with his cousin. He hadn't gotten over the incident, and was still upset and sad with what had happened.

A POEM FOR NICKY WALTON, A FRIEND

Yesterday, you were gone; today, I remember
Our first meeting over some jazz records.
We were young then, 14, 15, does it matter?
It was our adolescence, our youth.
It was spent well; we experienced life so
That as men we would feel our duty would be fulfilled.
The beer and the wine we drank then.
We thought we knew it all; of course, we were wrong.
You can't tell us; we're 15, and we knew it all.
The dance we went to, we would show off
And hope we would end up with a groovy chick.
Remember the chess games; you were much better than I.
I wish I could play you now.
Rich we weren't; money we had little,
But we showed them, didn't we?
Who needs money? We were cool.
Remember the car 10 of us chipped in and bought
And only one was old enough to drive?
It ran well for one day.
A whole summer we spent trying to get it to run a second time.
Yes, those were the days, school, football games, and parties at night.
Listening to jazz or old rock and roll, doo-wop, and blues,
We had our laughs and our tears,
But in the process of growing, we need both.
Remember your room with all the signs you stole.
No Parking, One Way, a traffic light,
And a Jersey City 300-year-old sign.
Yes, those were the days, the days of our youth.
Remember the fights; we thought we could kick everyone's ass.
That of course was, as long as our friends were around.
Where are those people now?
Joe, Mario, Rick, Walter, Howie, and your brother Mike,
I remember them all, but most of all,

I remember your mom.
She guided you, yet she led us all.
It was your house we spent most of our time at,
And to me, she was a mother away from my home.
Yes, those were the days of our youth.
But as the minutes turn into hours, hours into days,
We all got a little older and perhaps a little wiser.
You left for Maine to finish high school,
And I remained here.
Seeing you on vacation was great.
You were my friend and I yours,
And again I remained here.
We still crossed paths during vacations,
But now it was new.
Our heads were together, so we thought.
We grooved on life; people were beautiful.
Remember how you passed for Indian
When we all knew you were black?
If only you could know what I felt.
Color didn't matter.
But then it was our youth,
Long before life was beautiful.
Then it happened; high school was over.
The army called you.
You hated it; *peace* was the word, not *war*.
Where was that at? You couldn't kill,
But they wouldn't understand; they never do.
They only know how to take, never give.
It's a simple matter to say, "We don't want you, son."
Life was more important than to die for some belief you never had.
So you left, we got high for the last time, then Good-bye.
How were we to know it would be our last?
For on a cold day, you were home on leave.
The shots rang out, and in the paper I read,
YOU WERE DEAD BY YOUR OWN HAND.
I never knew you were home; maybe I could have helped.

You loved life, remember; it's too beautiful to lose,
But you made your choice. I knew you as only a friend could.
I believe that you always knew what you were doing.
Much knowledge gained as a youth I owe to you.
Without you as a friend, I may never have become a full person.
No matter how long I live or whatever I do or become,
There will always be a place in my heart and soul for you.
You will always remain a friend.

I wish you were still here, Nicky. I know we would have remained friends. I learned a lot from you, from music to the right people to be with, to be free, and to be an individual. Thanks so much for your friendship and for turning me on to so much including the music I may never have experienced.

NEXT . . . graduation, work, more music, school, and "the times they are a-changin'"

I graduated high school in June 1963 and got a job right away on Wall Street. It was easier to get a job back then, and I was not ready for college, nor was I even thinking about it. I went to work and made $65 per week—hog heaven. Worked with a guy named Johnny, and he had a close friend named Larry. Both were body builders and did contests as such, but, more importantly, they asked me and my girlfriend to join them and their wives to go to various New York jazz clubs. This was their once-per-month outing.

So more people turned me on to more live jazz. Ella Fitzgerald, Eartha Kitt, Louis Prima and Keely Smith, Miles Davis, and Gerry Mulligan, to name a few. We went to clubs like Basin Street East, the Blue Note, and the Village Gate. Another new world opened for me, and I enjoyed it to no end.

By 1964 to 1965, coffee houses were beginning to open in Jersey City, people were coming in to play music, play chess, etc. Sort of what was going on in NYC. I could play chess, enjoy the folk singers, have conversation, and share ideas along with meeting more new people.

I was still working, but had decided to take a few college courses at night. I had met a couple of people at one of the coffee houses who were also in college. They were spending a lot of time in Greenwich Village, and we became friends. Through them, I got to realize that college may be the way for me to go. We all hung out a lot, smoked our share of pot together, and listened to a lot of music. We laughed a lot and had a great time. I remember going with them to see the

Lovin' Spoonful at the Night Owl Café on West 3rd Street in the Village, prior to them ever having a record deal or radio play.

Music was getting a bigger push due to the British Invasion. The Beatles played at Shea Stadium. The Rolling Stones, The Who, and The Kinks were beginning to tour America. Also, the West Coast bands were getting airplay on AM radio. Then it happened . . . underground radio had arrived.

A NYC public radio station, WBAI, which had played classical music, was now playing all the music we wanted to hear, commercial-free. We got to hear all the folkies, rockers, East Coast, West Coast, UK, you name it. And it didn't matter if the songs were 20 minutes long or longer. It got played.

By now, given I had been turned on to pot, as I mentioned earlier, the music was even more intense. I got involved with the antiwar and civil rights efforts and had decided that I was going to attend college full time.

There definitely was a movement going on. Change was in the air, and the battle with the conservative establishment had begun.

Music moved the youth. Music made us listen to what was being said. Musicians played at the protests. We were one, and we believed if we stayed together, we would make change happen. We could end a war, and we could help equality for all. Conversations in college, even in night school, were changing, more were questioning authority. We had become more vocal on issues and more diverse. The cultural, social, and sexual revolutions were growing.

By 1966, I was a full-time college student. When I started that September, my hair was longer than those around me, over my ears. In fact, to my surprise, there were just two of us with long hair in a school of about 5000, right across the river from New York. We even had a lot of professors who had taught in NYC universities.

Was I in a time warp? To this day, I remember the remarks by other students, by teachers who were clear they would not call on me in class due to not being of the norm, whatever that was. Nothing like being the only one in class with a hand up to answer a question and not being called on. It was weird, but I still kept my hand up. This did get some other students a bit upset, and they made their point loud and clear, "Why are you not calling on Eddie when he has his hand up?"

Then my long-hair cohort cut his hair. Me, I was older than most freshmen and just went along, did my work, passed my classes, and put up with the shit. I had another life outside of school. I decided to see if I could work on the school newspaper and write a record/concert review. My idea was accepted, and off I went to my new writing career of sorts.

I was still hanging out at the local Jersey City coffee houses, and still going off to NYC to catch up with friends at various bars and coffee houses there. I was now 21 and I drove to NYC; no more subway for me. Funny, to this day, I still don't like taking subways. I must have had my fill as a kid, with my mom taking me to NYC and then my own travels as an adventurer into the Village (ha-ha).

THE STAGE BEGINS TO GET

SET . . . and now the joint, music, music, and the world begins to change for me

As I said earlier, coffee houses were starting up in Jersey City. One in particular, on Sip Avenue, became a hangout for me and a few friends. It was large enough to accommodate a stage, serve good coffee and desserts, and attract some decent entertainment, from folkies to small groups that played jazz and rock and roll. A good place to relax, play chess, and socialize with people on the same page. We were labeled hippies. That was cool. I guess we were hip, and we liked that.

Here is where I met a guitar player/folkie named Don Johnson. He sounded like John Stewart, who had replaced Dave Guard in the Kingston Trio. Stewart also had done a solo album, which I had, and here was a folkie playing his songs and playing them well.

Don and I had some coffee and good conversation, and I found out that he also lived in Jersey City. He played at the café a few more times, and we became friends. We smoked a few joints together here and there, and he was impressed that I could roll a very nicely shaped joint.

This led to an invite after one of his sets to join him in Greenwich Village and go to his friend Danny's apartment. He asked if I would teach them how to roll a joint. I thought this was pretty strange, but off we went. Free pot for teaching someone how to roll a joint? Okay, I'll bite, or smoke, so to speak. Danny lived on Sullivan Street, between Bleecker and Houston Streets, in the heart of things happening in the Village.

Well, this turned out to be more than pot rolling. I found out that night that Don and Danny worked with a NYC band called The Blues Project. The group had a loft above the Café Au Go Go, which was down the street from Danny's apartment. Café Au Go Go was a well-known club for music, comedy, and up-and-coming performers. Don and Danny had to go over there and asked if I wanted to come along. Sure, we were all very stoned. I had rolled them a lot of joints and spent some good time teaching. Yes, they got it down, and we smoked a lot to make sure they were rolled correctly and they burned nicely. They did. And off we went to the loft.

I had never seen anything like this place. Equipment was all over the place, drums set up, amps, organ, and synthesizers (had to ask what those were). Danny and Don did what they had to do, and I just looked around, amazed, and in awe.

Finally, Don explained that he was a tour manager/roadie, and Danny was a roadie. They then said they were playing the next night at a NYC college and asked if I would like to go with them, watch what they do, and hear some great music. They told me where to meet them and at what time. We met at the loft, and I went along with them in their truck.

This was the beginning. At that time I had no idea I had any future in the music world. I just knew I had some friends who worked with a rock and roll/blues band that sounded fantastic. I just couldn't stand around doing nothing, so I helped with unloading and loading their equipment in and out of their truck. I started working as a roadie, I guess, just by helping some friends. AND DON WAS CLEAR, "IF ANYONE ASKS, YOU'RE WITH THE BAND!"

Okay, I could do that.

THE MUSIC IS FOR YOU . . . glad to have been a part of getting the music to you, the audience

So here I was in 1966. I had the opportunity to hang out with The Blues Project, a band that was amazing, according to my standards. I had never been this close, backstage, out front, hanging out, and helping out. I was there early on as the fly on the wall during the early rise of the hippie music scene.

I stayed out of the group's way; just helped out Don and Danny. If they asked me to get something, I did. The Blues Project played the Café Au Go Go a lot. Easy gig, with the equipment just upstairs, in their loft. From here, I was introduced to a few new places to hang out.

The Tin Angel, across the street from Café Au Go Go on Bleecker Street, was a great place to have coffee, dessert, and meet people. It was a place where some of the musicians who were playing in the area also hung out. Next door and directly across the street was the Bitter End, another club that, for the most part, featured folkies such as Tom Paxton, Eric Andersen, Tim Buckley, Buffy Sainte-Marie, and Judy Collins, to name a few. The Bitter End exists today in the same place it did in the '60s.

Downstairs from the Tin Angel was the Dugout, a large bar. It had great beer and free peanuts, and we spent a good deal of time there, as did the artists who played in the nearby clubs. It was the place to get a drink, given the clubs that the artist played at did not serve alcohol.

By now, I had met so many people. My world was changing, as was the music and the politics. An awakening was going on, and it was spreading coast to coast and around the globe.

THE SHOW MUST GO ON . . . and
be the best one each time

Now that we established that rolling a joint can actually lead to something more than getting high, time to look at where it went.

Early on, I spent a lot of time watching the shows and doing a bit of roadie work, mostly at the Café Au Go Go. The Blues Project's first album was out, and the second one was on the way. The band's lineup consisted of Andy Kulberg on bass, Al Kooper on keyboards and most vocals, Steve Katz on guitar and vocals, Roy Blumenfeld on drums, and Danny Kalb on lead guitar.

I had never been so close to anyone who could play like Danny. I was mesmerized by his guitar leads. In the future, I would experience other great guitar players from very close up, too. Knowing and watching Danny prepared me for the guitar expertise of the likes of Eric Clapton, Jimi Hendrix, Mike Bloomfield, the Allman Brothers, and many, many more, including those of today and those still making me listen in awe of how good they still are, such as Lindsey Buckingham, Bonnie Raitt, and Bruce Springsteen, along with endless present-day guitarists who, without the prior mentors may not have achieved the same or better skills and may not be as good as they are today.

While The Blues Project wrote a lot of their own songs, they also did an incredible version of Chuck Berry's "Wake Me, Shake Me" along with a lovely version of the Donavan song "Catch the Wind," sung by Steve Katz. Everyone also was amazed at Andy Kulberg's flute playing on their original instrumental, "Flute Thing," which brought down the house. Andy would take you into another dimension, into another world of dreams. Al Kooper and Danny would sing some of the bluesy songs along with any originals written by Al. What an amazing experience I was having, which till this day, I can't believe I was there right in the middle of it all.

As an outside observer for a few months, I was able to get a real feel for what it takes to be an artist, be in a band, generate a following, and get paid for something you love. I didn't know then, but what I was seeing and not realizing and what I was learning was a huge help as I spent more and more time in the music industry on various levels over the years. In the beginning, it was fun meeting new people, meeting such talented ones, being, as I said, an outsider who had a chance to be on the inside looking out.

The music scene was beginning to explode in America. San Francisco had free concerts in Golden Gate Park, the Fillmore was open, the Matrix, and the Avalon Ballroom, to mention a few, all presenting bands from around the world, playing what the people wanted to hear.

This was not Top 40. This was what was called underground music. More FM radio stations were popping up, playing the music we wanted to hear and, in a lot of cases, get high to. We in NYC had the Go Go and the Bitter End, Steve Paul's the Scene, uptown on 44th Street, and Washington Square Park, which was filled with people playing music outdoors. The streets in Greenwich Village were filling up with more of "The Hippies" and many runaways who were trying to find themselves along with peace, love, and understanding.

I was now in my first year of full-time college. Luckily, I was at Jersey City State College and could drive to Greenwich Village, with no traffic, in less than a half hour. So when I had the time, I hung out or spent more weekend and holiday time working as a part-time roadie with The Blues Project. I still was a bit of an unknown to them. I was just Don's friend who helped out.

By 1967, The Blues Project was playing more shows. They were invited to play at the Monterey International Pop Festival with some of the top rock artists of the day, from Jimi Hendrix to the Mamas and Papas, to Simon and Garfunkel and Janis Joplin, among others. I was just a helping "hanger-on-er," so I was not invited to go.

When they returned from California, more area colleges began booking them. At one point, after a show in Pennsylvania, Al Kooper came over to me and asked my name. He had never asked who I was before. I had been around for a few months, on and off and on weekends. Al said he knew I was hanging out and helping with Don, but now he saw my name among the autographs that the fans were getting. A bit embarrassed, I told him that people had started asking for my autograph while I was breaking down the equipment. I explained that I had told them I was working with the band as a roadie, but they didn't care. They wanted my autograph, too. I then apologized, but Al just laughed and was fine with it.

So, I was no longer the fly on the wall. I was asked if I wanted to work with them. I told them I a full-time student, but summer was coming, and I could work for the summer and various weekends and school breaks. That seemed to be okay if it was all right with Don, which it was.

I was now a real roadie, at $50 per week and $5 per diem for food and expenses. I was now a real apprentice to what would become an 18-year journey.

What would come next—the bands, the times, the work, the people, and the scene? Now, I really was inside looking out, being part of the cultural change and political change, always watching what was going on. Being part of it, I believe it made me a better, well-rounded, and more knowledgeable person. Looking back, I believe what I was learning and experiencing helped me in college and helped when I took over the college newspaper from 1968 to 1970. I also believe that the years in the music business helped me become a better executive business coach, building relationships and helping presidents of companies become more successful in later years. (More on this later.)

Besides the colleges and various clubs, I was able to work at Murray the K's Christmas show. He was a local well-known radio disc jockey who even claimed to be the fifth Beatle. He put on quite a few weeklong holiday shows with multiple big-name groups. The 1967 show was held at the 68th Street RKO Theater in Manhattan. The headliners were Mitch Ryder and the Detroit Wheels along with Wilson Pickett, both with huge top 40 hits. The Blues Project was booked along with Richie Havens as local underground artists. Also, for the first time in America, British bands Cream and The Who were on the bill. Both had been getting quite a bit of airplay on the new FM underground radio stations.

These events ran for a week, up to eight shows a day, so we worked and worked and had a lot of fun. It was crazy—rush from the dressing room, do a couple of songs, rush off, move the equipment to a safe place, return to the dressing room to try to relax, and then do it all over again a few hours later. There must have been 10 acts, and this, as I said, went on for a week. It was my first experience outside the club scene and the college concert circuit. We shared a dressing room with Eric Clapton, Jack Bruce, and Ginger Baker of Cream. What great people to meet and hang out with.

Another Joint Story. We spent a lot of time hanging out, waiting for the next show. At one point, I remember sitting across from Ginger Baker as he was rolling what looked like a seven-to eight-inch cigarette.

"Okay, Ginger, what is that you are doing?" both Larry Waterman and I asked. (My longtime friend Larry was a full-time roadie with The Blues Project.)

Ginger looked up and said it was a joint, and we fell out laughing, "A joint?!"

"Yeah, have some," he replied.

Okay, we went for it. Seems the Brits roll joints with tobacco in them and sprinkle the pot along the tobacco. After that was done, we showed him a real American joint, rolled and ready to smoke. No nicotine, no waste of pot.

Ginger played great when their next set came up, and we all gave each other high fives! Eight shows a day wears one out, moving equipment back and forth and making sure your stuff didn't get mixed up with someone else's. Good fun, good laughs, and great to meet my first people from the U.K. Looking back, I am still amazed at who they were, and still are.

AND THE MUSIC PLAYED ON . . . as did we all

As a roadie, even part-time, while working, you worked full-time. It was not just sex, drugs, and rock and roll, the catch phrase that was used a lot regarding the musicians and those of us who were working for the bands. Yes, we laughed when we heard the line, but the reality was that the work was hard at times even if the group was doing weeklong engagements. Equipment had to be set up and repaired on the road. Speakers, drumheads, and guitar strings had to be replaced often. Then, if any of big stuff broke down, such as the truck or a microphone, guitar, set of keyboards, amp, etc., it was our job to get it fixed and keep it running, and be ready with back-up equipment if anything went down during a show.

I remember holding up a cymbal stand during an entire set. For 45 minutes, I sat under the cymbal, on stage with the drum set right next to me. My ears rang for a couple of days (more on this later). We all laughed, but the show must go on, and it was an important drum stand; we didn't have an extra one for replacement.

What about packing up a show and getting on the road at 1 or 2 a.m., and then driving hundreds of miles to get to the next gig? Once there, you set up again, and be ready for the band to do a sound check when they arrive, not to mention making sure the band members have their needs met in the dressing room, from food to drinks.

Also, many times at colleges, there was no stage, and we had to build one from platforms, if they were available. There were times over the years that we were glad at least to find a music equipment store in the town so we could get something we needed. Then, of course, there was the truck with all the gear and making sure it was not broken into or stolen, which did happen over the years. Nothing like being in the middle of nowhere, trying to rent equipment, trying to rent a new truck to carry it all in, and keeping the tour going if it did break down. Yeah, Hertz and Avis!

There were no real tour managers in the early days. Don was not only a roadie, he also acted as a tour manager and handled the money and the band, gave a hand with the equipment, and helped solve any emergencies that came up.

Yup, sex, drugs, and rock and roll. What a myth! Well, maybe not on days off, unless they were days that we just had to sleep.

In these early days with The Blues Project, there was a lot of experimentation with sound systems. Most clubs had them. The Café Au Go Go had a decent sound system for their 200-seat room. Most colleges found something that was adequate. But most bands didn't have one of their own, and, in the early days, there were only two large companies that were able to set up for big shows, one out of Boston and one out of San Francisco. These two companies took care of most of the theater and outside shows that came up. Another company, guitar-maker Guild Guitars, did some work with The Blues Project, creating better amps, especially bass amps. It had a lab in New Jersey where it worked with musicians to help get them the best sound possible.

My girlfriend at that time, "Dilly" Diane Dally, was working for the VP of Guild, who also was the son of the owner. Out of nowhere, she gave me a brand-new acoustic Guild guitar with a hardshell case. Besides "Happy Birthday," her words were, "Now maybe you'll learn to play instead of only playing air guitar."

Guild was sold years ago and is no longer family-owned. But I still have the guitar. It's a D-25 #285, a classic, worth a lot these days. That guitar ended up on quite a few albums of artists I worked with, given its great sound and the fact that it was readily available in the NYC area when there were no acoustic guitars to get a hold of quickly. Pig Iron, Elephant's Memory, The Stranglers, and a few other bands used it on certain recordings.

THE SHOWS CONTINUE . . . great experiences with other acts

Still with The Blues Project, I remember we played a show at a college in NYC, and we opened for Ten Years After from the UK. Amazing meeting and watching Alvin Lee play up close.

Then there was The Who, known for breaking their guitars, pushing over their amps, along with kicking their drum set off the stage. The first time we met them, The Blues Project opened for them at a NYC college. I remember Larry and I were in a panic, given that our equipment was still on the stage behind theirs when they were playing. We guarded our stuff very closely and ducked a few times. It was a very low stage, and we were on each side, trying to keep a watchful eye. We survived, as did the equipment. Backstage, I was kidding around with Keith Moon, The Who's drummer, and we both laughed, and he gave me his t-shirt. Wish I still had it. Larry got Roger Daltrey's. They were very nice people, no egos to deal with.

We all knew we had our part to make sure the show went on and went on well. We packed up and went back on the road to the next gig. Later that year, The Who and The Blues Project played for two days at the Fillmore East in NYC. With our equipment kept out of the way, it was great to see them again.

The underground was coming aboveground and being heard more and more. Music was getting stronger, jamming more, and the acts were getting more politically vocal about what was going on in the world. Groups were doing free shows around the city to support the antiwar efforts and the Civil Rights Movement; free speech was a must for all! Colleges now had a Students for a Democratic Society

(SDS) faction on campus, and, in many cases, they were shutting down the schools. There were the Black Panthers and various other groups being heard regarding freedom on all levels. And on the other side was the Silent Majority, as the nation's conservatives were called. But we rocked on!

I mentioned earlier a rock club on 44th Street called The Scene, run by Steve Paul. This place was becoming the uptown hip and cool place for bands to play. There, I had a beer with Jim Morrison from The Doors one afternoon. The band was packing up and leaving, and we were getting ready to set up for our few days of gigs. The two of us sat at the bar and talked about being on the road. He was from Los Angeles, and I had never been there as of yet but knew of the scene along Hollywood Boulevard. He discussed what was going on with some of the up-and-coming bands being played over the New York FM radio scene.

I did get to see him and The Doors again when I was invited to a show and backstage when they played in Asbury Park, NJ. I was and still am a big Doors fan.

We played a couple of days of shows at The Scene, and packed the house each night. The odd thing about this club was that it had no area on the side of the stage for any of us to stand and be ready if something went wrong. We had to sit out front, right next to the stage, sort of front row with the audience.

It was still 1967, and a few weeks later, *Look* magazine put out an issue called *Youth Quake*. *Look* was doing a photo essay of what was happening with the youth generation around the country, East Coast, West Coast, and in between. Lo and behold, there was a large black-and-white photo of The Blues Project on stage at The Scene, and there I was sitting in my seat against the wall paying attention, sitting right up at the stage, working but looking like a fan in the audience. I made it in the press!

We played at this club a lot, and Steve Paul, the owner, was a real good guy. One of his close friends was Tiny Tim, known for the song "Tiptoe through the Tulips." Tiny Tim was one of the nicest, oddest people I ever met.

There is one more memorable instance regarding The Scene that sticks out in my memory. We were unloading at The Scene when we went into the dressing room and found Tim Hardin, best known for his song "If I Were a Carpenter." He was on the couch with a needle in his arm and a very dazed junkie look on his face. He was definitely out there, and we just left him alone and checked on him often until he was able to leave.

Tim did no recording after 1973, and he died in 1980 after a long battle with drugs. Sad, he wrote such great songs.

So it goes, me, a kid from Jersey City, experiencing a slice of real life and still keeping the beat. I had no idea or any thoughts if I was going to be a survivor of the times. I was a big pot smoker and did my share of LSD once in a while, but that was about it in those days.

Then Larry Waterman decided to get married. This was a big deal. All of us involved with The Blues Project were overjoyed; this was going to be fun. Larry had met Dawn a few weeks earlier, and in those days, things happened on the spur of the moment. So they planned to get married in Central Park, on top of a very large rock, near the 5th Avenue side of the park. They would walk up the side of the rock, and we all would be standing there as guests and ushers. It took place in early 1968, on a very cold Sunday. Tiny Tim sang "Here Comes the Bride," and Danny Kalb of The Blues Project played it on his harmonica. Larry and Dawn got married, and, in a few weeks, it was over.

The *New York Daily News* put the ceremonial picture on the front page. It was a pretty big crowd. Some of our favorite followers showed, including Aviva and her best friend, sister of New York folkie

Eric Anderson, as well as club owners, bartenders we knew, and the rest of The Blues Project. All in all, it was fun, and the party afterward at the Café Au Go Go was one hell of a private party. You go, Larry! As an aside, I have heard from Larry in the past year, and he is now in Alabama with Dilly Dally, who is one of his oldest and dearest friends. It's great being back in touch, and thank you, Larry, for some help jogging my memory regarding some of the things we were involved with.

CHANGES ARE A-COMING . . . new experiences, new things learned for the future

The year 1968 was upon us. The Café Au Go Go was home base, and I worked with The Blues Project on and off, while going to college. With no traffic, I could be in NYC and Greenwich Village in 20 minutes to a half-hour. At night, the streets of Greenwich Village were filled with lots of hippies, runaways, and the decent, friendly police who were just trying to keep some semblance of order. Washington Square Park was filled with people playing music, smoking pot, doing acid, etc. Life was electric. Fillmore East was now in full force. Everyone who was anyone played there. Many new and up-and-coming acts were opening for the headliners and were hopeful that one day, they too would headline. I now was known by those who worked these places, so I was able to get into these shows without paying. Very cool perk.

As for college, I took over the school newspaper as editor-in-chief. This was a political move. I helped the two people running for president and vice president of the student government to get elected by getting the artistic, semi-hippie/hippie, and political folks to vote. I was asked up front what I wanted, and, given I was the present music reviewer and worked on the paper, I wanted the editorship. I got it under one condition: "Get the paper out on a regular basis," which we did.

We put it out every two weeks, got very political, artsy, and well read. There were 5000 students, and we were printing 10,000 papers every two weeks. By the time I graduated in 1970, we had won 23 national awards. We were not your typical college paper. We were more underground, but the college left us alone, including using language they did not approve of, but we only used it when we felt it was needed. It was cool with the president and administration (sort of).

Meanwhile, back to rock and roll. I was working a couple of times a month if I could with The Blues Project. Things were getting a bit hectic. Al Kooper had visions of starting a new group with Steve Winwood from the band Traffic. Al quit The Blues Project and left for the UK. The adventure didn't happen with Winwood, but what did happen was a great album with Mike Bloomfield and Stephen Stills called *Super Sessions*. It holds up even today and features a great jam on the Donovan song "Season of the Witch."

The Blues Project now had to find a new lead singer, which they did. However, egos were running wild. I remember working an outdoor show with them at Tompkins Square Park in the East Village. I recall it being a disaster. The new singer thought he ran the band, and Steve Katz and Danny Kalb did their best to keep it together.

I don't know the real story of the band's demise; I was back at school doing my student stuff. But I know that Andy Kulberg, the bass player, was getting involved with a new group along with Roy Blumenfeld called Seatrain. They recorded an excellent first album. The Blues Project broke up and I was offered a job at the Café Au Go Go for the summer of 1968.

ROCK AND ROLL IS HERE TO STAY . . . new views on what was going on musically and in the world

It was 1968, and the Summer of Love had arrived in NYC. Don and Larry were running around, trying for other road gigs, and I was now the guy at the Café Au Go Go's door on the street. Here I was on Bleecker Street, watching the crowd of people walking around, having fun, and crowding the streets. I was letting them know who was playing at the Go Go.

"C'mon down and join the show. Cream played yesterday, and Jimi Hendrix is on tonight. Get your tickets for Ritchie Havens on Sunday. See the greatest East Coast bands, West Coast bands, and the new acts you've heard on FM radio."

It was happening, and I saw it all. Then I said the wrong thing to Barry Imhoff, the Go Go's manager.

"Barry, I have to move my car."

"What?" he replied. "You have a car?"

My job changed. I was now on the day shift, and I was the person who went to the record companies and got the promo materials on the acts performing at the club. I also was the person who made sure the sound system worked, the acts got set up on stage, and that they got their needs met. If they were from out of town and needed other equipment, repairs, etc., I made the calls, sent their roadies to the appropriate places. I got to meet a lot of people, not only the musicians but also record company executives, A&R people, marketing folks, agents, and managers, along with many varied people involved with the artists in and around the music industry.

Good stuff, and I could hang out at night, listen to the music, go backstage, and meet more people. This was a fun summer, and I had great contacts for the future.

Then something else happened. Al Kooper came back from the UK and had an idea for a new group. He brought in Steve Katz on guitar, Bobby Colomby on drums, and Jim Fielder on bass (he had played with Buffalo Springfield). The Go Go became their place to put it together, rehearse, and get the rest of the players lined up. Al did it and did it very well.

It was a great opportunity for me to be able to see the growth of the original version of Blood, Sweat & Tears during that summer. I was working there every day, so when the club was free for them to rehearse, they did, and what a great first album they made. (Just an aside, I have my iPod on, and just as I typed in BS&T, on came "I Can't Quit Her" from the first album, with Al Kooper singing lead. Nice timing.)

So, with the Summer of Love came change. I watched it walk by the club and all around Greenwich Village, and I was part of it all. The Café Au Go Go was now the premier underground rock club in NYC. Everyone wanted to play there, and a lot of them got their chance.

On an off night, you may see Bob Dylan stroll in and do a set, or Van Morrison, Ritchie Havens, just about anyone who was around. Hendrix played for three days after he quit playing the opening act on the Monkees' tour. The Fillmore was beginning, as a larger concert hall. You could see Tim Hardin, Tim Buckley, and Eric Anderson on just about any night, across the street at the Bitter End. One could hang out next door at the Dugout and see various musicians having a beer.

I once smashed into Judy Collins when I ran into the Dugout to tell Ritchie Havens he was on at the Go Go. I'll never forget the bluest eyes I've ever seen. Ah, "Suite: Judy Blue Eyes."

Or, you could go upstairs to the Tin Angel, and, if you were lucky, you could get an outside table on the small balcony and watch the people flow by. You knew change was going on, and change was very active. Sex, drugs, and rock and roll, but I still had to work.

Next door to the Go Go was the Garrick Theatre, a small theater owned by Howard Solomon, who also owned the Go Go. Playing there for eight months or more was The Mothers of Invention, Frank Zappa's avant-garde band—incredible music, players, and a lot of fun to watch. The Garrick also was the last gig BS&T played with Al Kooper in 1968.

The summer ended, and I was back at school. I still had my connections with Don and Larry, who were working with the new BS&T, and I got a few gigs when I could. They were going through some changes, and it was beginning to get obvious there were some strong artistic differences. What the differences were, only they knew. Al Kooper was gone, and they hired a new lead singer, David Clayton-Thomas, and they became a more commercial-sounding group. They were the best-known horn group of the time, but others were coming up, such as Chicago, who was their main competition.

LESSON LEARNED: Of course, we all know that competition is good.

As the change took place and new gigs began to happen, I was lucky enough to still hold on to my temp roadie position with BS&T. I did a few shows while I was still in college. I got to share a room with David, given he had some arguments with Steve Katz regarding his wanting to play more guitar. So they stuck him with a roadie, me.

I remember one instance where Steve made it clear, "I'm the guitar player, and we hired you to sing." (David was a very good guitar player, but you know egos). I got to hear "Spinning Wheel," a song that became a big hit for BS&T, which David wrote. In fact, I heard it so much that I still hear it if I think about it.

Wherever we traveled, we encountered the anti-hippie, anti-youth movement, which was growing. I remember one instance after we played at the American University in Washington, DC. All went well until the next morning when we were in a diner, trying to have breakfast before driving north back to NYC. Besides not getting our order taken right away, there were a few "suits" at the counter, making rude comments about us, our hair, and who we thought we were. Finally, David got up and grabbed the attaché case from Don, which held the fee from the show the night before at the university. He walked over to the counter, suggested that they shut up, mind their own business, and opened the case and asked them, "How much do you assholes need to leave us alone?" He had about $10,000 in the case. BS&T was beginning to get some good solid fees.

Then, as the summer of '69 approached, a few things happened. BS&T was getting more and more airplay, and I was asked if I wanted to go with them to California. Why not? School was out. I had never flown nor been to California. Off I went. WOW, a plane to San Francisco. We got the equipment with Don and Larry at the airport, found the hotel, checked in, and sorted out the gig at the Fillmore Auditorium. We were the opening act for Eric Burdon and the Animals.

Was this a dream? Nope, reality. We had two days off once we got there, and after we got all of our gear from the airport and got ready for the Fillmore, we had some time to roam around Haight-Ashbury, Golden Gate Park, and get a good feel what the summer of love and the San Francisco scene was all about. And it was about Peace, Love, and Understanding, end the war, and all people are equal. This S.F. was incredible, and a lot of people were jammed all over the place.

Pot smell was in the air, and it was very obvious there were a lot of folks on acid.

During one of the days I had off in San Francisco, I ended up in Sausalito, right over the Golden Gate Bridge. I was asked by some friends of mine back home to get their leather jacket that they had left at a house a few months earlier. Little did I know that my friends back home had ripped a couple of people off that lived in the house they sent me to. Somehow, I became friends with a couple of the people there. Turns out, John Villanueva, whom I'm still friends with, was whom I needed to talk with to get the jacket. He was a roadie for Santana. Long story short, I invited everyone to the show at Fillmore. They came, and later on, I stayed at John's house for a month, just hanging out in San Francisco. John went on to co-manage Journey and now is retired in Hawaii. Nice way to go, from roadie, to management, to being part of the team that created the video screens that are now used at large events. You go, John. Glad we're still friends.

We were New Yorkers, and this was Cosmic California. Well, we had to work, so it came time to get the equipment set up and lug it all the way up a huge flight of stairs to the auditorium. We had some help from some groupie girls who were outside, and we promised them a free pass for the show. Off we went to work.

I do remember a pretty funny instance with the groupies. One who was carrying a drum case asked me my sign. "Cancer," I answered. She dropped the case and said she was not going to work with me, and off she went.

I knew that folks in California were into astrology, but I had never encountered this behavior. One learns something new each day. I did get my chart eventually done a few years later when I moved to San Francisco for a year. At least I could talk a bit about who I was astrologically as long I was going to be in that part of the world.

The shows went off without a hitch, filled to capacity. A great way for BS&T to start a West Coast tour, playing San Francisco, then Los Angeles. We played S.F. for two nights. One night after the show, when we were back to our hotel, I was outside by the pool, maybe 2 a.m. or so. I was taking it easy, away from the band and my fellow road crew buddies, just sitting, smoking a cigarette, when up came Eric Burdon. He asked if he could join me. Sure, and we had a great time just bullshitting about the road, San Francisco, and all the stuff we experienced for the first time in California. Nice guy, cool hanging out with him. They went on to their next show as we did. We went off to a week in Los Angeles at the Troubadour.

Next, the Troubadour club on Santa Monica Boulevard in Los Angeles. What were we going to find here? The Buffalo Springfield, The Doors, Crosby, Stills, Nash and Young, and more? The Hollywood scene? The Troubadour is a wonderful place. We enjoyed the week. Many people came to see BS&T.

Another instance comes to mind. I was asked by the band not to let anyone in the dressing room. Nothing new with that. As they were getting ready for their set, along came this guy who wanted to see the band. He was very insistent. We went back and forth, me saying the band was busy and was not seeing anyone until after the show, and him not getting that.

Finally, he says, "But I'm Neil Young."

I replied, "Nice to meet you, but still no entry."

He went away, and I just stood there, a bit in awe but doing my job.

We had a comedian open for us, Murray Roman, during the two shows a night we did for the week. Larry and I had settled in. We knew all we had to do was turn the amps on and off, so stupid us decided to do a little acid. Not a full dose, just enough to get a nice buzz.

We were sitting in front of the stage, ready to jump up and get things set once Murray was done with his shtick. Then all of a sudden, he reached over and grabbed one of our glasses of water. He then went into a comedy bit on we had dosed him with acid. Doing some outrageous contortions, he scared us so shitless that we ran out of the club with the audience laughing at him and maybe us. We were glad we had a few minutes to compose ourselves given we had a bit of work to do. It was a very memorable moment, you had to be there.

Another memorable moment was when BS&T was set to do the *Steve Allen Show* and was at the studio rehearsing. Jimmy Fielder, the bass player, was going out with Laura Nyro, who was an amazing singer-songwriter, and BS&T had recorded one of her songs for their new album. I was asked to drive her from the hotel to the studio. No problem, we knew each other. So off we went. We decided to put the radio on, and to our surprise, there she was, singing one of her songs from her album. It was the first time that I was in the same place and time with an artist sitting next to me and on the radio. We both laughed, she had never heard herself as of yet on the radio.

California was now over. It was a great trip, not only for BS&T, but also for me. This was a new experience, and I learned a lot for future use even though I didn't know it then. We headed back home.

Given, I was doing some gigs now with the new version of BS&T, and they had a new album coming out with David as lead singer.

We began a series of gigs at La Cave, a small club in Cleveland. Obviously, I had ended my Café Au Go Go gig to go to California with BS&T, and Barry Imhoff understood that BS&T needed my help for a bit. He was cool, and we remained in contact, especially when he went over to manage Fillmore East.

Off to Cleveland we went. I'm not sure how many weekends we played there, at least most of August. I remember one trip especially.

We had done a college gig in NYC and, when it ended, Larry and I packed up and hit the road at 1 or 2 a.m. We were off to Cleveland, about a thousand miles away, knowing that the sound check was going to be around 3 or 4 p.m. later that day.

So we drove. At the same time the 1968 Democratic convention was being held in Chicago, and there was a lot of unrest, protests, marches, and arrests. We had work to do and little did we know that some of this was going to spill over onto us. No riots, but it was very hard to get gas for the truck. All everyone saw were two long-haired hippies. They put us in the group of rioters, and we didn't get a lot of service. We got cursed out, hassled, and spent an inordinate amount of time looking for gas, coffee, etc.

We made it, very tired, very hungry, but as I said, the show must go on and go on perfectly. We couldn't wait to get back to NYC and safety.

Another encounter with BS&T was in the late fall of 1968. I had done some odd gigs with the band and still was friendly with Don and Larry along with Bennett Glotzer, who was the manager of BS&T. The band was getting a shot at appearing on *The Ed Sullivan Show*, a very well-known weekly variety program on Sunday nights. Ed had had the Beatles and the Rolling Stones and most of the top new music acts that were taking the country by storm. BS&T were set to perform. It was a great show, and afterward, I was invited to the after show party at Bennett's office on 57th Street.

While walking up to the door of the office, I heard a voice say, "ED, can you help me?"

Out of a cab that just pulled up was Laura Nyro. I hadn't seen her since we were in Los Angeles. She always wore long, flowing dresses and wanted me to help her up the stairs so she wouldn't trip. What a fine lady, friendly, and a great talent. I never ran into her again, and a few years ago, she passed away.

During the party, Bennett pulled me aside and asked me if I wanted to join the band for a world tour. I said I was honored, but I was going to stay in school. I had been the one who chose to go, and I planned to finish. He understood and thanked me for the job I had done and he knew that school was important to me and graduating was my goal.

School was calling. I learned a lot over the few years connected with BS&T. Looking back now, I realize how much and how helpful it all was with my future endeavors with other artists.

MORE TO COME . . . meanwhile
back to college

I was now running the newspaper. I had a lot of work to do as I was a junior. I had some offers to work with BS&T when I could, which I did. Most of the time that year, I was doing schoolwork, being political on campus, and running the paper.

Besides odd jobs with a few groups here and there, summer was coming, the summer of '69. I needed a job and began to ask around, leave messages, etc. I got a call from Sid Bernstein's office. He and Billy Fields were managing a group called Rhinoceros, sort of a super group, but no one called anyone a super group in those days, at least not yet. Anyway, they were looking for a tour manager. Would I be interested? Sure. I knew who they were. They were getting a lot of play on the FM stations with an instrumental called "Apricot Brandy."

Rhinoceros was made up of Billy Mundi, drummer from The Mothers of Invention, and Danny Weis, guitar player from Iron Butterfly. Also, from a Canadian group, there were John Finley, on lead vocals; Michael Fonfara, on keyboards; and Alan Gerber, on bass. Other band members came and went, but these are the members I knew and worked with.

These folks were wonderful to work with, very little egos going around. They all lived in a very large mansion on Mahopac Lake, upstate a bit from NYC. I don't know who gave them my name, but a job for the summer was needed, and this was a blessing.

There was a lot of talk about a big three-day concert called Woodstock, and Rhinoceros was hoping to play, given they were getting so much airplay and they had well-known members in the group. Until they were given the thumbs up or down regarding Woodstock, there were a lot of shows booked for the summer. The band traveled in an RV and had roadies and a sort of ex-tour manager who was useless, but who lived in their house and raised guinea pigs, a room full of them. He was no hassle to take over from. So off we went.

Lots of fun shows, great music, and, as I said, good folks to work with. They made my job easy. The roadies were on top of it and realized I had come from their world and understood the show must go on, go on time, and everything had to work perfectly.

I remember a show at the Boston Garden. We opened for Iron Butterfly. It was pretty cool, given that Danny had been involved with their biggest hit "In-A-Gadda-Da-Vida." If I remember correctly, Danny jammed with them on the song. Very cool! I also remember playing the Asbury Park Convention Hall. Then, when I got back to school, someone came up to me and asked if I was the guy they saw on stage. Pretty cool, too!

Then there was the very large show at the New York World's Fair building on Long Island. It was where they had the New York displays back in 1964. For this show, Steppenwolf was the opening act, and there probably were up to 6000 people. This is where I had to hold up a cymbal stand for the drummer, Billy, for most of the set. I sat under it and got a bit deaf by the time the roadies fixed one up. Yes, more of the show must go on and you do what it takes to make it so.

We also had an opening act called Ten Wheel Drive. An excellent group with a great horn section and a fabulous singer named Genya Ravan. I ran into Genya a few times recently at a holiday party given by May Pang (more on her later). It's great hearing her sing, and she recently released a new album. She's performing and has written a book about her memories. Glad to know that she is still at it and, from what I gather, doing fine. Much success to you, Genya!

I remember another situation where we were playing an outdoor show at a mall playing on a flatbed truck as a stage. When the show ended, I was standing on the stage, talking to one of the roadies. We looked out at the audience and saw someone getting beat up. The guy getting beat up was unable to defend himself. Both the roadie and I jumped off the flatbed stage with mike stands in our hands and threatened to use them if this didn't break it up. It did stop, and we stood there until the beaten guy got help to get out of the way. I've never done this before, but you had to be there. Someone had to stop this. We had just done a very good show, and it was a great day. This was ruining it. Where was the peace, love, and understanding? It was 1969. We were supposed to be cool!

The next big event, or *supposed* to be the big event: Woodstock. We were told that the band was wanted for the show. We had the call. The truck was loaded at the house at Mahopac Lake. We were ready to go and make the drive. All we needed was the okay from Billy Fields and Sid Bernstein.

But no call ever came.

Instead, Sid Bernstein had booked the band to play at a high school prom on Long Island for $3500, versus the $1500 being offered to play at Woodstock. Besides all of us being bummed out, Rhinoceros should have been there, given the acts that were playing. We were part of that scene. We were known. Later, we found out that Sha Na Na took our place.

Also, to make a long story short, and to the best of my knowledge, on Monday, the band fired Fields and Bernstein.

LESSON LEARNED: It is not always just about the money. One must take into account what is best for one's potential future opportunities for success.

The next few weeks were not fun. People were beginning to leave the band and go to other places. Alan Gerber was off to the West Coast. He gave me his sheepdog that was so big, we had a hard time fitting it into my VW convertible. I gave him to my brother, who in turn got him to a farm where he had plenty of room to roam.

This was the end of my Rhino days. The band made some change in personnel, recorded another album, and then I assume, went their own ways, to other groups. I never ran into any of them over the years until recently, when I had found John Finley on the Internet. We had a great conversation and he sent some new music he recorded. He sounds better than ever. As for the rest of Rhinoceros, I do hope they are all well and enjoying life. They were some of the nicest, talented people I had ever worked with.

Then, with the summer gone, I was off to my last year of college. I had learned a lot over the last three to four years regarding the music industry. From the live shows, to recording, to learning how a venue is run, from 200-seat clubs to concert halls and college concerts, both indoors and outdoors. A lot of knowledge and I had no idea what I would do with it. Graduating college, running the newspaper, and being a student leader were my main goals now that graduation was approaching.

I was still friendly with Rhino when I was back in school for my last year. They had some new members, but they still did me a favor. When the Kent State University shootings happened on May 4, 1970, I as a student leader, along with others, thought our campus needed to be shut down in protest. The deal we made with the college president was that, given it was finals time, those who were good with their grades up to that point could stop going to classes and those who needed to take their finals could. We said we would not stop them.

We also got the okay to plan a day of live music, speeches, and whatever else was needed regarding what was going on, not only at

Kent State, but also pertaining to the peace movement worldwide. We set up a stage, got professors to make speeches, and I got Rhinoceros to come to Jersey City State College and play for free. They played on and off all afternoon. School was shut down except for those few who were taking their finals.

Thank you, Rhino folks. Thank you, professors who spoke and others who helped out. We had a very peaceful all-day demonstration, not only against the war, but also against the horror that happened at Kent State.

As for a **Joint Venture** with Rhino: They always carried a half-pound or more pot on their tour bus, and given we all could roll a joint, we had contests to see who could roll the best one. We all won, and all joints worked and were smoked readily.

Finally, as an aside, the band Santana had played at Woodstock, and I had a couple of friends working with them. I had met them when I was in San Francisco with BS&T. When they came to NYC for a few days after the Woodstock festival, I took John, the conga player and drummer, on a car tour at 2 a.m., with the top down, through all of Manhattan, including a ride on the Staten Island Ferry.

LESSON LEARNED: Relationship-building has it merits.

SCHOOL DAYS . . . golden rule
days, what's next

Being a senior now, things were quite busy, not only with school, but also as editor of the school newspaper. We were quite political. I also had to decide what I was going to do once I graduated. I still was involved with some of the bands and musicians, but was working very little with them.

Once I graduated in June 1970, a bit of panic set in. But I soon got lucky. I got a call from Gary Van Scyoc, whom I had met a couple of times. He was the bass player with a band called Pig Iron, and they needed my help. They were doing shows around the East Coast and in the Midwest. I met with the band and took on the job as tour manager. A few of these folks would show up again in a few years. I'm glad we worked well together.

The biggest show we did was at Soldier Field in Chicago, with Leon Russell, Iggy Pop, and many more. This was an all-day festival, and maybe 50,000 people were there. Good fun, Pig Iron played early in the day, so we had the rest of the day to watch the show and mingle with whomever was backstage. However, by the end of the summer, there was some friction internally with the group, and I decided that I needed some money, so I took a substitute-teaching position in Jersey City.

While I was substitute teaching, I did some weekend work with a group called The Albert, named after The Albert Hotel in NYC. I knew the girlfriend of the trombone player, and they needed some help once in awhile. This led to working a gig after a day of substituting at a high school in New Jersey.

All went well until I left with the truck full of gear to head home. I was stopped by the police in the school parking lot. They wanted to search the truck and search me, which they did. I had to unload the entire truck by myself, and lo and behold, they found some pot in a shoe under an amp. I was told that some student said he got his pot from someone in the band, and I was the last to leave, so I was the likely suspect. The group had just played a week in Vermont, and one of the guys must have put the pot in his shoe and left it in the truck by accident.

In short, I got busted. The trombone player came back from NYC to bail me out. I got a lawyer, and by the time it was all over, the court appearance, the fines, etc., it cost me $500 and no record. It was a hard case to prove. Given the pot was in a shoe, it was a tiny amount, and the judge just fined me. So that was another **Joint Venture**, one I could have done without.

School was out and summer came. Hooray, no more subbing! By the summer of '71, I was off on a trip to camp around the country with a couple of friends who were also teachers. We landed in California, both Los Angeles and San Francisco. I knew some people in San Francisco, so we had a couple of places we could stay. This led to me moving to San Francisco in search of work.

I had a friend, Marty, and we moved in together. Marty had some money, and we decided that we could produce rock shows at a wonderful venue called Bimbo's. (More on Marty later.) This was a wonderful 1940s-type venue, with multi-level seating, a good-sized stage, and a dance floor. We did a few shows, no great success. We produced It's a Beautiful Day and the new lineup of Big Brother and the Holding Company (sans Janis Joplin, who had gone solo).

I spent almost a year in San Francisco and when this venture ended, I moved back to Jersey City, sometime in early 1972. So what was going to come next? I couldn't go back to substitute teaching. Besides hating it, I was a terrible sub. I'm surprised I never got fired.

THE NEXT BIG THING . . .
I got rescued, hooray

I couldn't have been back from California more than a couple of days. I was in need of sleep. I had driven from San Francisco, nonstop except for gas, to Jersey City. I vaguely remember it taking about 60 hours.

So, here I was at my parents' house, fall of '72, when the phone rang. It woke me up, and on the other end of the line was Gary Van Scyoc from Pig Iron. He asked what I was doing and did I want to go to work. He had a job for me as a tour manager with a group called Elephant's Memory. I had never heard of them.

However, half awake, I knew I needed to get work and generate some income. We agreed to meet the next day at a rehearsal studio in the West Village, where they kept their equipment.

I still knew nothing about this group, but I knew Gary, who played bass, and Adam Ippolito, who was on keyboards, also from Pig Iron, and I trusted them both. So off I went. All the band members had arrived by the time I got there. Usually, I was talked to by one or two people from a band or their management company. But it was obvious that this day I would be interviewed by the entire band. Been there and done that before, too.

I was then introduced to Rick Frank, the drummer, and Stan Bronstein, the sax player, along with Tex Gabriel, the guitar player. It was clear that Rick and Stan ran the group, and they asked most of the questions, basically about what I did in the past and then what I would do in certain situations. All went well, and then they asked me if I had any questions.

I asked about who managed them. I was told Leber and Krebs management. And how were the gigs going? Were they planning any tours, and what was up with future recordings?

Then I got the biggest shock of my life so far. I was told they were the backup band for John Lennon and Yoko Ono. They were, at times, referred to as the Plastic Ono Elephant's Memory Band. WOW.

I got the job, and I was starting right away. First up, I met the road crew, who showed up after the interview. They were very competent, and their sound man also was a bit of an electronics genius and could fix just about anything. They were getting ready for supporting their second album, *Elephant's Memory*, which had John Lennon playing guitar on some tracks, who also produced the album on Apple Records. They also were set for a couple of months to work recording and backing up Yoko Ono on her upcoming album, *Approximately Infinite Universe*, produced by John Lennon. This was being done at the Record Plant Studios in NYC.

I met Jimmy Iovine, who was an assistant engineer at the studio. He was young, focused, and you could see he was very much into production as well as engineering. Later on, he became very influential in the music business, to say the least, from productions to starting and owning one of the top record labels in the world. My pleasure to have met you. (Jimmy shows up again later.) I also met a lot of people at the Leber and Krebs office. They had just signed Aerosmith to a contract based upon the fact that they were selling out 7,500-seat arenas in the Boston area. I also got a good look at a larger management company. It paid off later on, but I wouldn't realize that until years later.

EXCERPTS from a 2002 interview with *PSST! Magazine*

I met everyone in the group, and we immediately went to work. Unfortunately, I had just missed the One-To-One benefit concert run by Geraldo Rivera for the Willowbrook Institute (bummer), but things were getting busier. John and Yoko were cohosting a week of *The Mike Douglas Show*, and Yoko was thinking of doing her own album. The band itself was getting lots of offers to perform all around the country, so we were on go.

I was a bit nervous for a while, with all the hype and hangers-on that were around everywhere. Jerry Rubin, the Hell's Angels, and anyone else who thought they could have their own, personal Beatle, made it their business to be there all the time.

There was always a lot of energy and tension in the air. Looking back, it's no wonder John drank a lot and got crazy for a while, left Yoko, and ran off to California. At one time, there were so many hangers-on that when the band played solo gigs, things got a bit hairy. Trying to get the show going meant I had to empty out the dressing room and get people moving. Well, try and move a couple of Hells Angels who don't feel like going anywhere. Needless to say, I learned a lot about tact. I also discovered that quite a few of the Hells Angels could be real helpful when things got crowded and we needed some space.

September 5, 1973, the band appeared at the Hells Angels' Pirates Party held on a ship, the *S.S. Bay Belle*, together with the Jerry Garcia Band. The Pirates Party was later featured in the 1983 documentary film *Hells Angels Forever*. This was an incredible show. It was a benefit show run by Geraldo Rivera. It was an all-day boat ride around Manhattan Island. The Hells Angels from New York and California were the guests, and watching their motorcycles pull up was amazing. I got to meet quite a few and found them to be not only interesting but also quite a bit of fun, given they were in their own group and only had to deal with each other. Sure, a few got tossed into the Hudson River and there was a bit of pushing and shoving, showing off some ego. All in all, it was a great ride, great music, and a chance to meet some of the Angels who showed up at our shows once in a while. I knew I was cool given I worked for the band, and there was always an Angel asking if he could help, and, at times, the help was needed.

Once Yoko began her first album, things got really interesting, especially around the studio. John would show up and work on the production with Jimmy Iovine, but he was a kid then, as I said, very talented and a real nice guy. He treated the people who worked behind the scenes extremely well.

Yoko was totally focused on what she wanted and made it clear to all of us that she was there to work. She fed us well—it was my first taste of sushi—she treated us well also since we all had to do our jobs. We worked with the equipment, did business, and kept the hangers-on out of the way. I got very friendly with May Pang, John's secretary. Of all the people around there, she was the best. No ego, no bullshit, and she got everything done.

Some of the other people working for Yoko or the record company, including the photographers, were, for the most part, a real pain in the ass, especially when we had work to do. Quite often I had to step in and chill out the roadies when they got in everybody's way.

At times, there was a real sense of paranoia. I remember waiting for two hours at John's Bank Street apartment for him to decide to come out and give me a guitar that Yoko wanted to use in the studio. Even Yoko's secretary, who was there, didn't make a move to get him to come and give it to me. I didn't care what he was doing, and after a while, I made enough noise knocking so that I did finally get the guitar. All of us who worked with John and Yoko were sort of like bodyguards who had to protect them from whatever it was they were worried about. It slowed everything down an awful lot.

One really great night, Mick Jagger, John, Yoko, and Carly Simon showed up for a priceless jam session. We would just hang out and groove. I'm sure, somewhere, Jimmy Iovine has a tape of it. But things also could get ugly. Some nights, John and some of the band and I might end up at a bar on 91st Street called HOME. Ritchie, the owner, and John became great friends. It was a great little place to hang out. I remember having to drag John out physically to get him back to his apartment—he was living at the Dakota then—before he got too drunk and started to make trouble with the patrons and their girlfriends. John liked to hit on women when he was out of his mind. But he usually listened to me and let me take him home where the doorman would get him up to his apartment. I was glad when he cleaned up his act and got together with Yoko and their son. It was that act that helped me decide to stay home years later with my own three-month-old and take care of him for the first year. We bonded in a way that only people like John and Sean could truly understand.

Life was crazy in those days. People lived under enormous pressure and egos were exploding everywhere. Everyone thought they were important. Watching the wannabes was fun, until they got in the way of those of us who had to do our jobs to make sure the show went on. And no matter what, we made sure that the show always went on.

BACK TO THE ADVENTURE . . . on to the studio

The recording studio was where I met John and Yoko for the first time. Shook hands, nice hellos. John made a couple of funny comments that we all laughed at, and it was off to work.

I had to make sure the roadies and everyone had the equipment they needed. The sessions were starting around midnight, so it was going to be a long night for my first time around John and Yoko. They went off to work quickly. Once everything was in place to get started, the road crew and I sat around doing a lot of nothing until someone needed something. John came out of the studio a few times to take a breather, make small talk, and then went back to work.

I have always been amazed how John was able to keep anything together. So many people wanted a so-called piece of him for whatever their personal gain may be, even if it was just, "I'm friends with John Lennon."

No wonder there were times that he locked himself in his room at his house. They also had a few personal assistants around. I became friendly with one in particular, May Pang. I'm still friendly with her. She was John's assistant and was the only one who worked for them that seemed to get whatever John or Yoko needed, and quickly. I counted on her especially during the studio time. She was great, and still is. Thank you, May. You know what I think of you, my friend.

Some of the others around them always seemed to be letting their egos run wild. Always too busy to get anything done when John and Yoko needed something. I never knew what they did except hang around. They must have had something that they did. I was much too busy to deal with them. As far as I was concerned, they were in the way, especially when recording was going on.

The session went on, and it was obvious that Yoko knew what she wanted, how she wanted to sound, and what she wanted the album to sound like. One may not like what she did her on albums, but she was very impressive about what she wanted.

Back to the band and shows we were doing around NYC, New England, and the Midwest. A lot of shows in NYC, colleges, clubs such as CBGB, out to Long Island to My Father's Place, and one can't forget Max's Kansas City. In the Midwest, we did colleges, from Iowa to Wisconsin and in the Chicago area. We did the regular Midwest touring that everyone does. We had very good crowds. I think people thought at times that John might show up, but he didn't.

I remember a gig with the band in Ann Arbor. It was '60s activist John Sinclair's birthday, and we had a cake for him. Well, it soon became decoration for the dressing room as the party turned into a cake fight. It was a nightmare for the road crew, trying to protect the guitars and amps from the flying frosting. And it was rough collecting the show money, given the damage done. But I got it, with no damage money given back.

Too bad Elephant's Memory was one of the hardest bands to work with. Their egos soared just because they worked at times with John and Yoko, but this was no reason to be as demanding as they were. They had no big hits, although they got some decent play with a song called "Mongoose."

There also was a lot of coke going on with Rick and Stan, along with tequila and scotch. I do remember a few times how hard it was to get them on stage and get the show on go. Once, at Max's Kansas City, Rick was so done in from coke that his nose was bleeding during the entire set. I was glad it was not my job to change the bloody drum heads.

One of the biggest problems was the arguments and fist fights that Stan and Rick would have prior to going on stage. Amazing the time and energy wasted along with their talent. They were excellent musicians but attitudes, egos, and plain trying to be what they were not—STARS—got in their way.

A couple of years ago, in 2009, I was interviewed by a woman named Judith Furedi for her book, *John Lennon: In Their Own Write*. A very nice book, and it was a pleasure to discuss some of what I did when I was with Elephant's Memory and my John Lennon interactions.

Interview from *John Lennon: In Their Own Write*

Interview with Ed Kleinman, tour manager of John Lennon's back-up band, Elephant's Memory

JF: What was your first encounter with John Lennon?
EK: Around 1972, right after the One to One concert at Madison Square Garden.
JF: Do you recall any interesting or funny anecdotes about John?
EK: Sure. He had a tendency to come out of the studio, make jokes, and expect us to laugh even if it was 4 a.m. and we had been around for hours. I also remember sitting in his living room on Bank Street for hours, to decide to give me a guitar that was needed in the studio for Yoko's album. When he was living uptown at the Dakota, driving him home once in awhile when he was under the influence of who knows what, alcohol or whatever were quite funny. It was the '70s, so good laughs.
JF: What was the most memorable or notable incident you recall?
EK: Getting him out of HOME restaurant before he got in trouble and in a fight with some jerk due to having fun the jerk's girlfriend. Who he was, held no weight. Into my car we went and off to the Dakota, dropping John at home.

EK: During those days, he was not very serious—at least not when I was around. This was the time he was doing a bit too much of everything, yet his serious side can be seen in the bed-in and *The Mike Douglas show*. He cared especially about world peace and did something about it, including putting his stay in the States on the line. So whatever he did to release himself from what I call the NYC Beatle, where everyone seemed to want a piece of him—from the groupies to the media—even the Hell's Angels learned to respect him. We were all part of NYC. John somehow got through this period, but with that kind of pressure for such a long time, it was amazing that it all came together with having his son, Sean.

JF: What were the typical things he would say or do?

EK: He loved giving the peace sign to everyone.

JF: Where were you when you heard the news about John's murder?

EK: I was in London doing business for the band The Stranglers when my wife called me to tell me John was shot and killed. I was in shock. How could this happen?

To this day, I wonder what magic he would have created had he lived. I'm still friendly with some of the band members of Elephant's Memory and with May Pang. When I see them, various memories come to mind. From the inside looking out some more.

By 1974, it was time to move on. The band was having problems, and I got an opportunity to try my hand at management.

EVERYONE . . . and anything can happen, the good, the bad, and the ugly

I had been friendly with a local Jersey City group called Everyone. They had a large following and were playing pretty consistently. We worked out a deal where I would do some roadie work along with them, run the sound, and also act as their manager. They knew my history, and it was my first chance at trying my hand at managing a band. This was around 1974.

The band wrote nice pop songs, had great harmonies, and were all good looking. On stage, they presented themselves very well. They had a bus for their equipment, a sound system, and good amps, gear, and guitars. They also rehearsed at a friend's house with plenty of room, about an hour outside of Jersey City. The house belonged to Lenny DiNicola, who was a dentist and a friend to us all. We had all graduated from Jersey City State College.

Everyone was a five-person band: two guitarists, Puggy and Freddie; Tommy on drums; Tom on bass; along with Steve on keyboards. They worked well together, with very few disagreements, and all of us pitched in to get the gear set up at gigs. We worked as a team. They played the bar/club circuit around New Jersey, so work was not the issue.

The issue was to get them seen in NYC, seen by people who could possibly get them a recording contract.

At some point in early '75, Steve decided to leave the band, and they had to reform now as a four-piece group. We all had and knew a professor named Ray Arlo who hung around with us a lot. He had a place in Woodstock, NY, and offered to let us stay there, rehearse, and get everything tight as a four-piece group. This turned out to be one of the best things that could have happened to Everyone.

Once they got it tight, we were able to get a few shows at a great bar/restaurant in Woodstock, called the Joyous Lake. This place was well known for showcasing local/national acts as well as serving good food.

Bearsville Studios also was in the area, and everyone from Bob Dylan, who lived in Woodstock at this time, to The Band, The Rolling Stones, John Sebastian, Orleans, and many more, including, in the past few years, the group Phish, recorded there. Bearsville was owned by Albert Grossman, who managed Bob Dylan, The Band, and Janis Joplin, along with Todd Rundgren. He often ate and watched the shows at the Joyous Lake along with doing a lot of production at Bearsville Studios with unknown, new, upcoming, and established bands.

Well, we got lucky. Albert Grossman was in the audience when Everyone played one night at the Joyous Lake. This was the very first show they did as a four-piece group. When the show was over, I got a card from Albert Grossman, saying to give him a call, which I did. Everyone was asked to join Todd Rundgren to do some demos with him at Bearsville Studios. This was very far out, a start in the right direction. We had never done any professional demos, and it was great to have a few songs recorded and to be able to use them with record companies to try and get a recording contract.

Nothing came out of the sessions other than some well-needed studio experience with a known producer. But we were very positive. Bottom line, we had a few songs recorded and now had well-done demos. The stay in Woodstock ended, the band was tight as a four-piece rock-and-roll group, and it was time to get back to local shows and see how the fans liked the new set up.

First place I could think of for Everyone to play in NYC was a restaurant/bar called Home on 91st Street and 2nd Avenue. It had live music at times, and I knew the owner, Ritchie, quite well from the Elephants/John/Yoko days. He liked what I played him and set up the first show. I was able to get a few record company people to come, too. I wanted some outside feedback to see if I was on the right track.

Of course, the Jersey crowd of fans showed up, and not only was there no room inside the place (it was a small place, and the band had to set up in the window and on the floor in front of the window, it also got very crowded on the street.

Glad for the nice weather. It was springtime, and things went well. Everyone sounded great and had fun. The audience inside was a mixed group of New Yorkers and Jersey fans. Ritchie asked the band to come back, and we set up a series of Tuesday night gigs for a few months. This was perfect; they could be seen and heard, and being in NYC, I was able to get various executives, A&R people from record companies and agents, to come, listen, and give feedback. Over time, they were seen by quite a few people.

I had Jimmy Iovine come by, who liked them enough to invite them to do some tracks at the Record Plant, where John and Yoko had recorded. We did some demos, which were great and were quite needed in our library. I was able to get them out to some record company people, but no bites yet.

Then Dino Danelli and Gene Cornish from the Young Rascals saw them and brought them into Electric Lady Studios in Greenwich Village. This was where Jimi Hendrix did a lot of recording. Everyone recorded some demos with Dino and Gene, who liked the demo but were not ready to move forward with a recording deal.

We also spent a lot of time at a studio called Sound Ideas in mid-town NYC. I was friends with Thom Ianniccari, who was an engineer there and who liked Everyone a lot. He would bring us in during late night off-hours, and we were able to do a lot of recording. The band was getting a lot of studio time and a lot of experience in that arena.

Some of the feedback the band got was to let Puggy do all the lead singing. He had the personality, the looks, and a great lead singing voice. He even got to audition for the Davy Jones role on a family TV series due to Jones' leaving. The band balked strongly, and both Freddie and Tommy wanted to sing the songs they each wrote. Trouble was brewing. They were adamant about this and stood their ground. I explained that getting the deal was more important on who sang the lead on the songs. If a deal was struck, they would all benefit from publishing, album sales, and live shows. This came up a few more times; again still no resolution.

I had a good relationship with an agent named Jon Podell. He booked the Allman Brothers, Crosby, Stills, Nash & Young, Alice Cooper, and many more. He had his own independent booking agency and did well. We struck up a deal that he would try what he could to get Everyone a recording contract. He had seen them, liked them, and saw that he may be able to make a bit of money from a deal. That is all he wanted to do: Make the record deal and collect a percent. That was it.

Well, Jon came back with a four-single deal on Columbia Records. After all the rejections and tries, this was a good deal. If things went well, an album would be next. I brought this to the group, and they were very excited. Things were going to move forward.

A few days later, I got a call from Jon, who wanted to meet. Sure, I guessed he had more info and more details. I went to his office, and he said he wanted to speak face to face. He said the band had come to him and requested that he manage them, not me. He said that he told them that if "Eddie is not going to be the manager, the deal is off."

I appreciated his support and told him they had said nothing to me. Also, if this were the case, I would let him know the outcome as soon as I spoke with them. It was clear that I was most likely done with them. So, Everyone and I had our conversation. It was over and they were free to go their own way without me. But Jon had kept his word, and they were unable go with him either.

I had spent two years with Everyone, and what I experienced with them was what I call fear of success. They had an opportunity, a chance to start to record for a major label, and I probably could have arranged for Jon Podell to do some booking since he was going to make some revenue from record sales. The band passed on it all and, to this day, never got a record deal.

The only one still doing anything live with music that I know of is Puggy. He does a Neil Diamond impersonation show at supper clubs. I'm still friendly with him, and it is too bad he was never able to go solo with his music. He is a good guy and was the only supporter for the Columbia deal with me as their manager.

That was the bad and ugly, and I still think it was a stupid move on their part. I've seen it over the years. Sometimes, you only get one shot and, if it looks good, you should take it and go on your adventure. You never know where it can lead. You know where doing nothing goes—NOWHERE!

LESSON LEARNED: As far as I know, Everyone never tried again on their own or with a new manager. That was sad, given they had the songs, the vocals, and the stage presence. But they didn't have the desire or the commitment, and maybe they didn't believe in themselves. One needs all three to succeed. They obviously were comfortable where they were.

MOVING ON . . . to the unknown and some surprises

I wanted to get off the road, if possible, and found myself working for Robert Middleman, who was managing a group on Columbia Records named Jerome Brailey & Mutiny—a funk band with Jerome having been the drummer for Parliament-Funkadelic. This got me off the road, and I learned a lot, mostly what *not* to do.

However, I met a lot of people from various record companies that I had not previously encountered. Robert was not a great guy to work for, and after about six to nine months, I was gone. I had met some people over the years, from management companies, record companies, booking agencies, along with a few lawyers and accountants (they would come in handy later on). So I spread the word.

I picked up some work with a group called Undisputed Truth, in early 1977. They had been a Motown act in the early '70s, and now due to various changes in their personnel lineup, they had a new album, *Method to the Madness*, to promote. I got my friend Thom Ianniccari to do sound, and along with a couple of roadies, off we went. Their new lead singer, Taka Boom, the younger sister of well-known R&B artist Chaka Khan, was now taking up the charge to get out front and show the audience what they were all about. This was their comeback tour. They had some airplay, and the shows they were doing were mostly colleges and a few multi-act shows.

One of the shows in Cleveland had various artists on the bill, including Michael Jackson in an early appearance as a solo performer. When it was his time to go on, no one could find his sound man, so I volunteered. I didn't know his music, but I knew enough about the sound system and the board that, with the help of my sound techie Thom, we got the job done without a hitch and got a big thank you from the people working with Michael.

Once we got back to NYC, I was done with Undisputed Truth. These folks didn't get along at all, and I didn't need to be working with people like that. Another, been there, done that.

Then, out of nowhere, I got a call from a woman named Mary Beth Medley. She was working with a management company run by Peter Rudge. They had The Who and The Rolling Stones for US touring and other business aspects, and Lynyrd Skynyrd, 38 Special, The Dingoes, and few others worldwide. I have no idea where she got my number, but she asked if I was available to tour manage a new group they picked up called LeBlanc & Carr, who were based out of Muscle Shoals, AL. LeBlanc & Carr had just released an album and was getting ready to tour. I was rescued again.

When I got to Peter Rudge's office, it was clear that they were the ones who were hiring me, not the band, which was great. It was something new, and the connection to this company was quite good. A few of these folks, Mary Beth and Bill Zysblat (their accountant), would play a role later on in my career.

Off I went to Muscle Shoals to meet the band and begin what was going to be an experience that none of us involved on any level are ever going to forget. We got to know each other, and the road crew was good about the new kid from the North coming on board. I was getting to be adopted as the new Southern Boy. The band was having a hit with a pretty love song called "Falling." The shows we were doing were from colleges to auditorium-type venues, such as Fillmore, to very large clubs that would bring in known artists (similar to the Bottom Line in NYC).

The funniest thing about this group was Pete Carr, who was one of the best guitar players I had been involved with. He played on stage with his back to the audience, and none of us could get him to do otherwise. He seemed to be a bit on edge once he hit the stage, but that was the way it was, so basically we all began to ignore it. Lenny LeBlanc was the lead singer, and he had no problem relating to the audiences.

Then the big break came. LeBlanc & Carr were set to go on a world tour starting in September 1977 and ending in February 1978, in Hawaii. We were going to open for Lynyrd Skynyrd, who just released their album, *Street Survivors*. The reviews were fantastic, and they were getting more airplay than ever. Once the tour began and I saw and heard them live, I was very impressed. I became a huge fan of theirs and began to really like what was called Southern Rock. We heard their music on the radio all the time, especially "Free Bird," but in person, it was incredible. They really had their act together, on stage and off. They were nice people to be around, and their road crew worked well with ours to keep things moving along.

Street Survivors was to be the one to set up Lynyrd Skynyrd as a worldwide-known band. But it came out three days prior to their plane crash, where six people died: three members of the band, Ronnie Van Zant, Steve and Cassie Gaines, the assistant tour manager, Dean Kilpatrick, along with the pilot and co-pilot. Ironically, the *Street Survivors* album cover pictured the band standing amid flames, which was quickly changed and re-released without the flames.

My experience with what happened was as follows. It was around the fifth show of the tour, October 20, 1977. LeBlanc & Carr had opened for them in Miami. And then Lynyrd Skynyrd was off, flying in their chartered plane to do a show in Greenville, SC. We were driving and headed off to meet up with them at the Louisiana State University in Baton Rouge to continue the tour.

Back in those days, you didn't get much on the car radio, if anything. So, it wasn't until we reached the hotel in Baton Rouge that we heard from the desk clerk about the plane crash. We then began getting calls not only from Peter Rudge's office, but also from many of our own families, loved ones. We were fine except saddened, shook up, and stunned. What happened? We had no idea as of yet.

I remember, to this day, backstage at that last show with them in Miami. Cassie Gaines, who was a background singer and Steven Gaines' sister, crying and screaming for the band to let her go with the truckers. She did not want to get on that plane. She did not want to fly. May she rest in peace with the others who passed away.

This was my saddest day on the road and, when I think about what had happened, I still can't get Cassie and what she was going through backstage that day out of my head. Too many artists have passed away, too much talent gone. Many for no reason at all and long before their time.

Peter Rudge was devastated, and the cost to him was unreal. For now, there was no work available from his office.

I was able to pick up some tour manager jobs after working with LeBlanc & Carr. One was with a singer-songwriter called Franklin Micare. He was a solo artist, living in Greenwich Village, and needed someone to help with getting things running at his shows, from his stage set up, to the sound, to dealing with the promoters. Easy, he had two guitars and an amp. Sometimes there was no need to take the amp given the venue had one. Nice guy. We were doing a couple of months' tour across the states, ending in San Francisco.

We were playing a couple of nights in a very nice club in San Francisco as an opening act for Leo Kottke, an unbelievable guitar player. This was a treat for both Franklin and me. I had invited my old roommate from my past San Francisco venture. Marty came with his girlfriend and, when the show was over, they came back to the hotel with me to get a late-night snack.

When we got to my room, I asked if he could wait a minute while I did some quick accounting and put away the night's fee from the show. I got a bit hung up looking for a lost 25 cents in my accounting. We had been on the road for two months, and this was the first time I was off. Yes, I could have taken a quarter out of my pocket and put it in with the rest of the money, but that was easy. I wanted to know where I had added or subtracted wrong.

Well, to make a long story short, Marty was hungry, as was I, so we finally did toss in a quarter after I had spent 45 minutes trying to figure out where I erred. After the late-night snack, we said our good-byes and promised to stay in touch.

The next day, Franklin and I left to get back to NYC. (More on Marty coming up later.)

PUNK'D . . . and on to a new world and a very new adventure, moving Fast Forward

It was now 1978, and I got a call from Mary Beth again. She wanted to know if I wanted a job with a group called The Stranglers, a punk band from the UK who were coming over to do their first US tour and were in conversation with A&M records and a producer called Martin Rushent, who was working on mixing a forthcoming album here in the States. They also were going to be booked by Ian Copeland, president of Frontier Booking International (FBI). Ian is also the brother of Miles Copeland, chairman and founder of I.R.S. Records, and brother of Stewart Copeland, the drummer of The Police. They seemed to be in good hands. The Stranglers were coming to the United States in support of their upcoming album release, *Black and White*, and to see if there was a market for them here.

I met The Stranglers for the first time at JFK Airport. This was in the spring of 1978. There were JJ Burnel, the bass player; Jet Black, the drummer; Hugh Cornwell, the guitar player and lead singer; and Dave Greenfield, the keyboard player.

They knew I'd be picking them up. I don't remember if anyone was with me, but I don't think so. I was on my own, and the driver to get us to their hotel was outside. As for their equipment, that was in the hands of their roadies, whom I had not met yet. They got off the plane with small carry-on shoulder bags. When I said my hellos and suggested that we get their luggage, I was told very bluntly, "This is our luggage."

Okay, a six-week tour and they had very little with them. I learned later that they wore black pants and black t-shirts and washed them out after the shows. I believe they had two to three changes in their bags. At least I didn't have to worry about baggage.

I got this job due to some people I knew at A&M and some people that were from Peter Rudge's organization. No problem. I had Itineraries for all and I knew where we were going and how. They kept saying various things that, at first, I thought were rude, especially coming from people who had no idea who I was and that this was their first time in the United States. However, I came to understand they were just testing me as they did with a lot of people they met and worked with. They did this to see if people would and could deal with them. I had no problem. I thought I was dealing with a punk version of Monty Python, so I just laughed and did my job.

That attitude paid off later on. It helped dealing with the road crew, keeping them on track, and making sure the shows ran well. The band got their needs met, and I laughed a lot with them, at them, and behind their backs. As I learned, using their terminology, they liked to take the piss out of people.

They were set to do some recording prior to the tour at the Record Plant in Midtown Manhattan. I had been there before, so this was not new place for me. I knew my way around, which was good. Now it was my time to be tested. They asked me to get a certain type of tea, all the past *Hustler* magazines, and a certain kind of Campbell's tomato soup.

Okay, the *Hustlers* were easy. We were in Midtown, 8th Avenue near 42nd Street, and there were a lot of porno bookshops in the area. The tea I got at an upscale market called Balducci's, in the Village. Given I was unable to find the specific kind of tomato soup that they wanted, I brought back the phone number (that was given to me at Balducci's) for Campbell's international head of sales, who said the soup was only made for export to the UK and Europe. I guess I passed my test and gained some more credibility.

Again, I thought this was pretty funny, but I was used to getting the job done, whatever it was. So far, these guys were easy compared with what I had experienced from other bands. The tour went well and, upon our return to NYC, we found that the band had a lot of tour support money left. I was able to get the record label to send the four of them back on a SST jet aircraft. After a three-and-a-half-hour flight, they were home.

More credibility, leadership as a tour manager, and the band knew I got this done all the way to the end of the tour, and we said good-bye.

There was talk about a European tour they were getting ready to do, but they were clear that even though I did a great job, I had never been to Europe. Regardless, a week later, I had a ticket to Glasgow, Scotland, and I was now The Stranglers' world tour manager.

I found myself throwing people off the stage, which I had never seen at a concert before. I got used to that and along with people in the audience spitting at the band as praise from the fans. This was new to me, but I was getting a bit *Punk'd,* so to speak.

This was strange, but the show must go on, and it did. This was in the summer of '78, and the tour went from the UK across Europe, including three shows in Yugoslavia. Amazing. Lots of countries, big arena shows, and varied types of currencies—the Euro was not yet invented.

We had 54 people on tour, from lighting, to sound, to drivers, to security, to our own catering company so we could eat what we wanted, when we wanted. They were great. They took orders from the band and crew on what they wanted for dinner, what they wanted during set up, for lunch, and for breakfast. It sure made things easy and helped the tour run more smoothly. We didn't have to depend on the promoters for anything in the way of food or drink. Smart thinking!

During the tour, we had a week stopover in Yugoslavia while the band went back to the UK to do some recording, leaving me in charge of the 50-person crew, an interesting situation. I had never been in charge of such a large group on tour. No worries with the catering company, unless they needed me. The drivers and security were cool and were helpful when I needed them. But I was concerned about the road crew, including one woman on the tour, who was a lighting engineer.

We all stayed at a hotel on the Adriatic Sea in Yugoslavia. There were three shows scheduled in Yugoslavia, and we had done only one so far. The hotel was very good-looking from the outside. However, once inside, the place was like being in a rundown Woolworths. The furniture in the lobby matched the plastic stuff in the rooms. My recollection was that Yugoslavia was all a front; behind any door was junk and rundown junk. You knew something was up with the country when they would not accept their own currency in their casinos.

The hotel had a big swimming pool outside on the edge of the Adriatic Sea so you could swim both in the sea and in the pool or just lounge around at poolside. Our woman crew member was the first for me to deal with, not so much with her, but the hotel. She liked sunbathing in the nude. It was good with me. She had a very nice body and was in great shape from climbing up and down lighting poles.

She took offense when told to put her clothes on, an argument ensued, and I had to step in. The only way I could calm her down was to offer her an extra day's per diem, 10 bucks. Not sure if I was set up by her, but with all the long-haired crew with British and Aussie accents along with me, the only American, we didn't need to get thrown out of the hotel.

There were other issues that arose, and this one, I got our security to help with. Alcohol of any kind was very cheap, and I had a lot of drunken roadies on my hands. Luckily, they stayed out of trouble, found bars in the area to hang out in. Also, if they were too large of a group, I made sure one of the three security people who were on tour went along. The drivers of the semi-trailer trucks and tour buses (we had two of each) understood what I was doing and were very supportive. They had been on tours that were much larger, such as the Rolling Stones and Led Zeppelin. One even was Keith Richards' personal bodyguard on a few tours.

Anyway, we got along very well and became friends. They knew what I had to do, so when needed, they were there for me. I was still a very firm believer in "get the job done, get it done right, or get out of the way."

The crew knew that I would send someone packing if they caused too much of a hassle and couldn't do their job. I accepted varied drunken crew members over the week as long as they were no hassle. No fights, but some sloppy behavior, so what? They were off, had their week of expense money, and knew that the next two shows in Yugoslavia were on the weekend and they'd better have it together, which they did. They, for the most part, knew I could do their job.

What I wasn't very good at was doing and setting up the lighting. I could direct, but not run them. The rest of being a roadie was no problem. The crew realized I had come from where they were. I had gained credibility and respect earlier in the tour, helping throw people off the stage—and this happened at every show, part of what was going on in the punk world. Also, at one of the UK gigs, I got a bit tired of being called The American, "What does he know?"

They didn't do it to be nasty, but just to see how I could take getting the piss taken out of me by them. To satisfy a couple of the roadies, I took over the sound for the show, did my job, looked at them, and said, "If I have to do your job, then why do we need you?"

I laughed and they got the joke and pretty much left me alone to do my job and were helpful when I needed them to do certain stuff. I now was the Good American who surprised them and fit right in. It didn't take long to be a team. When they needed something—repairs, new equipment, problems with the promoters, the venue, whatever—I got it done for them so the SHOW GOES ON PERFECTLY.

Portugal also comes to mind on this tour. The venue was a 20,000+-seat arena, a bit north of Lisbon. The country didn't get many shows, so this was sold out and more. The concert goers were coming early, and there was a crowd gathering, having fun waiting for the doors to open. Everything was unloaded, the crew was setting up, and the trucks were now parked outside. (They were able to drive in and unload, which made it easier for the crew.) I went to the venue a bit earlier to see what was going on and if the crew needed anything. I saw the crowds, and we pulled the car into the arena.

HOLY SHIT. The crew could not get enough power to run everything. I spoke with the promoter, and all he did was make excuses. We wanted him to plug into the power in the street, which we knew could be done. We found out that, at a prior show, they had tapped into that power. But, for some reason, the promoter was refusing to do it now.

The band showed up for sound check, and we clued them in. They started to see if they could use fewer amps. No way, the venue was too large. We tried using less light in the place, not only ours, but also the venue lighting. Nothing worked. The more we tried, the worse it got. The show had to be cancelled.

Outside, the crowd was huge. In talking to some of them earlier and prior to any known problems, I had learned some of these people had come from Spain, Italy, and other countries. It was summer, easy to travel, and people wanted to see a show and wanted to see The Stranglers. Some had paid a lot for their tickets and travel expenses to get there.

Then a riot started outside. People crashed the gate after they saw the tour bus leave and the trucks with the gear leave. Even then, they didn't know the show could not go on. We were able to pack up the gear and get the trucks on their way. The band tried talking to some of the crowd that had crashed the gates and began filling the room. Given there was still a little gear on stage that was getting packed into the last truck, the group tried to calm down the crowd that was growing inside the venue. No such luck. The last truck finally got packed and left the arena.

Word spread fast that the show had been cancelled, and the crowd started throwing rocks at the arena. We who were still there began to run out the back, and run for our lives! We were able to get out the back of the arena, and we could see the mobs rushing in. A lot of them chasing us. We ran across a big field behind the arena and into the various streets and neighborhoods in the area. We ran in all directions, hoping for help to get back to our hotel. We were in a very suburban area, all single-family houses.

A couple members of the crew and I ran up a street, with people behind us throwing rocks. We saw a door and knocked; no answer. We then tried the door, and it opened. We burst in, slamming the door behind us, and you could hear the rocks hitting the door.

We were all out of breath, and we looked up. There was a family of about six people who had been having dinner and were now staring at us and looking frightened. We were some sight that just burst into their house. I'd be scared also.

They were very nice when they realized that we needed help. They called the police, and we were picked up. We explained to the police what had happened. They knew about the riot at the arena and drove us back to our hotel. We were rescued! Only one crew member got hurt, and he was in the hospital getting taken care of.

Later that evening, the promoter came to apologize to us. One of the crew punched him out, after I was able to get money from him that was due to us. None of us could wait to get to the next shows. This was scary, and we were very thankful nothing got broken, stolen, or anyone else got hurt.

On to the next shows. Keep the tour going. We had done Spain and Portugal and still had Italy (two to three shows), Austria, Germany (three shows), Switzerland, Czech Republic, Belgium (two shows), Holland, and a few more I don't remember.

In Germany, I had a surprise for the band. The spitting was still a bit weird for me and it was happening at all the gigs. Also, at times, JJ or Hugh would jump off the stage and go after someone who threw a bottle or empty beer can (to show "more love and respect"). So, with the help of one of the record company execs, I was able to find water pistols for them to use and soak the audience back. This lightened up the place a bit, and everyone had a good laugh. They were used throughout the rest of the tour. Less jumping off the stage and less fighting with the audiences. Leave it to The American to come up with something (ha-ha).

I found additional interesting things to deal with in various countries worth mentioning. In Yugoslavia, the police would, with their assault rifles, line up in front of the stage and look out at the audience. I was the one to get them off to the side. However, they were not going to leave the venues.

In Italy, we did a couple of shows and were paid in Lira. It sure took a long time to count the Lira that they collected at the door and put into pillowcases. I got handed a couple of pillowcases to dump out and count.

Going from Italy over the Alps to Switzerland was incredible, and we had the driver stop and let us out to look around when we got to the top of a mountain. Holland was flat, and I used a bicycle to go from the hotel to the venue. Here, the fans threw their half-full beer bottles in appreciation, and we stopped the show to explain to the audience that this had to stop or there would be no show. It got better, and we all ducked more efficiently.

Germany was not my favorite place. It was like everyone screamed at you. Even the TV weather person demanded that it was what it was outside, even if it wasn't. I got very upset when I found one of our keyboards missing and then found it in one of the trucks that belonged to the TV station that we were doing a live show for. This was in Munich, and I got into a big argument with some of the TV station crew regarding our keyboard. I lost it and called one of them a Nazi. Germany was not for me, a Jew. Munich must have been leveled during World War II, since everything I saw looked new. We did our shows, and in Munich, we even played at a hall that was used by Hitler for speeches.

Then off to Antwerp, Belgium. It was quite interesting, checking out the legal Red Light district. I had seen the prostitutes walk the streets in NYC, but here they sat in windows with red lights on, interesting and legal.

The tour was mostly very good, a few hiccups, but it's only rock and roll, and we like it.

When we got back to the UK, we settled up all accounts that were outstanding from various shows, shook hands, and we all went out to dinner and had some good laughs regarding various things that had happened on the tour. I let them know that I was available if needed for any future tours. Lots of thanks and I flew back to NYC very satisfied.

Regarding what I took from the tour, the size of it, from the arenas to the amount of people involved, to the different cultures, many lessons were learned, which I was able to use later on.

LESSON LEARNED: Besides the show must go on, it was evident that it was only a numbers game. If you play small venues, you use less equipment. The amount would increase based on where you played. More gear, bigger stages, bigger audiences, just numbers. You had to perform at your best, no matter what.

The summer was over, the tour was over, and I was home. However, soon after I had returned home, I got a call from my friend Marty from San Francisco. (Remember him? I said he would show up again.) After our hellos and how are things goin', Marty came out with, "How would you like to have your own management company?"

"Huh?" I replied.

He said that anyone who could take as long as I did to find 25 cents the last time we were together may be a good investment for him. That began our conversation. He wanted to know what it would take and how much money he would need to invest. I let him know that I knew a good lawyer and a very high-end accounting firm that had a lot of experience and some very top clients. Barry Platnick was the lawyer I liked. As for an accountant, Bill Z from Peter Rudge's office had gone on to open his own office and was doing the accounting for a lot of groups, including the Stones, for America. I had good relations with both of them. I told Marty I would get back with him shortly. I set up appointments with both Barry and Bill.

First I met with Barry, and we worked out some details that would have to be presented to Marty. We decided that, given Marty was going to put up the finances, he would get 51 percent of the company; I would get 49 percent and control. Marty would not have any say in the daily running of the company given he had no experience in the music industry.

Then I went off to Bill, who advised me to get about $200,000, if possible. Then we discussed the fact that having access to that much money could be a disaster for me and I could find myself spending it foolishly. So we came up with a plan. Bill would be my accountant. I would draw a weekly salary and have my expenses paid. I would have to come to the office to get paid, hand in my receipts, and get any other checks that were needed after I explained what they were for. I would not have a checkbook in my possession. The salary we came up with was $175 per week, which was fine in 1978. Rent, phone, and other expenses would be paid.

I then got back to Marty. He said he would fly in, meet everyone, and if all went well, we would be on go. I let Barry and Bill know when he was arriving, and we set up a meeting to see if this made sense and if it were possible. It was.

We came up with and agreed that the investment would be $175,000. The salary and percent of business, along with me running it, was all fine, and in a few days, we had an agreement signed. When Marty got back to San Francisco, he transferred the investment to a bank account set up under the name Fast Forward Ltd. We now had an entertainment management company and needed artists for our roster.

WE MOVE FAST FORWARD . . . and
now we are in business

So now the challenge began. Where was I going to find clients to manage? First, I got in touch with Jerome Brailey. I knew he had left Robert Middleman. I was not sure what he was up to, but it was worth a try. We had a good conversation. He let me know that he was due for a new album on Columbia Records called *Funk Plus The One*. He had the tracks done, but needed help with the label, touring, and management.

We discussed terms, and he signed a three-year contract with me. Ian Grant, one of The Stranglers' past managers, also asked for help with a couple of his acts when they came to the United States, and he had an American group that needed a bit of care. This also gave me an opportunity to meet more recording industry people and get the word out that I had my own company.

Jerome came up to NYC, and we met with Columbia to get the ball rolling. It was a good start.

I began to realize that there were acts out there that were looking for new management, or had none at the time but had record deals. So I began to spread the word with various booking agents, my lawyer, my accountant, club owners, and various other friends and acquaintances who were plugged into the music industry. At the same time, I was working with Jerome and Columbia to get the album out with decent promotion. Jerome had his band together, and they were in rehearsals to get the music tight. A few times, Jerome had to come to NYC for some press set up by Columbia, and this gave us some face-to-face time since he was based out of Virginia. We began to talk to agents to get a tour booked.

This was the end of 1979 and into 1980. Jerome was beginning to do some new tracks in Miami, and with only a few performances going on in and around his home state, I was beginning to feel that he was having problems regarding touring. Did he have the right musicians, and did he even want to tour? Our struggle began. I needed him to tour and support the album.

I had to interview some groups as well. Amazing what some unknown acts with record deals expect from a manager. I walked out on a few after they were so obnoxious, rude, and just plain stupid. To this day, none of them ever seemed to get anywhere.

Then I got the surprise of my life. I had kept in touch with The Stranglers and had let them know that I had started my own artist management company. Well, the phone rang, and lo and behold, it was JJ and Jet. "What's up, guys?"

After the hellos and how-are-yous, they asked if I would be interested in managing them. I was in shock and asked them quite a few questions regarding their management, Dai Davies and Ian Grant. Seems that there were a lot of hassles and that Dai, being the main manager, was holding up a lot of money. The recording company, EMI, also was holding up a lot, and the band felt it was time to move on.

Why me? They felt that I had kept things together, made things happen, and they had respect for me. So smart-ass me asked them, "Can you guys still play?" (It had been a year or so since we last worked together.)

They laughed and said they were going on a UK tour, why don't I come over and see for myself and we can talk further, which I did. I knew I needed a lot of information regarding what they were facing, involved in, from not only their now-becoming-ex-managers, but also from the record company along with any unknowns that I may have not been told. I already had a pretty good idea why monies were being held up. They had multiple solid-selling albums, but they also had various arrests, poor dealings with the press, and who knows what else.

I spent a week with them on the road. They were performing better than ever and had some great new material. They were going to release a new album called *The Raven*. We discussed the hassles they had been having with their prior management, which had been holding up money of theirs due to the split. I also found out that EMI also was holding a lot of money that was due to them from record sales worldwide. I spoke with the record label and then with the lawyer they had. I also spoke with John Giddings, who was their booking agent and got some more insight into what was really going on. I spoke with my lawyer, Barry Platnick, as well.

I then sat down with the band and explained what I had heard and that the record label was interested in the band having new management, but also wanted the band to get their act together, so to speak, and start acting smart, not smart-assed, not kidnapping anyone from the press (as they had done and then left the guy out in the middle of nowhere) and not getting arrested.

So, the big question was whether they were ready to get more serious and start being cool with the press and do what has to be done to get back on the charts, get more support from the label, and pay attention to management. I let them know that I understood that they needed a good lawyer and new accountants that they could count on. I said I would have my lawyer come over, and we would find them the best that was available for them to make changes, but only if they were okay with whom we introduced them to. It would be their choice.

They said yes, and I sent for Barry, who came to London, and we put it all together. The record company saw that we were professional and released their money. Barry knew lawyers and accountants and set the band up with the law firm that handled Liz Taylor for Europe, for one, and a very strong accounting firm. The lawyers helped them with my agreement, which was very fair. I took 17.5 percent of everything that I worked on, from future albums, tours, and publishing. Also, once signed, I fired their old lawyer. A deal was struck with their old management company that everyone agreed upon, and that was over.

I then went with Barry and sat with the head of EMI and a couple of A&R folks, explained what we had done, and that it was a new road the band was taking. They were pleased. Barry went back to New York, and I stayed a few more days to make sure all was in place. They seemed to like the professionalism of the new lawyers and the accountants, and that made them feel more secure. It was good due to the fact that I now knew I could get answers regarding what was going on and, if the band needed something, then I knew it and was on it.

The Stranglers had a tour coming up, which John Giddings was setting up. I worked with John and made sure that the road crew was set. All was good, they went on tour, and I started managing them from the United States. Every four to six weeks, I was on a plane to London, spending a week at a time managing them directly. This gave me time to meet with EMI, John Giddings, and their lawyers and accountants, if needed, to deal with various issues that had come up. I got the latest updates on the press and promotion and how the album *The Raven* was released only in the UK and Europe. It reached # 4 on the UK album charts, and the single "Duchess" reached the top 20. Good start for a new management team, I thought. The travel was getting a bit maddening, and I found myself flying over to London from NYC at night and going right to work. Sleep came later.

I began talking to the band about another US tour. I was able to get I.R.S. Records to put out a compilation album called *Stranglers IV*. It was 1980, and I wanted a shot at the US market. They had only been here once, and it was a fairly successful tour, but there was no album out and nothing in the way of marketing.

I.R.S. said they would put out this compilation album, which included a few tracks from *The Raven*, which was already getting some play on college stations. Frontier Booking International (FBI), headed by Ian Copeland, was ready to do a national tour, and this was going to get us to San Francisco and Los Angeles then back across Canada. It was all beginning to come together, and the band was behind it.

My now-wife, Susan, who then was my girlfriend, came to work with me as the tour and press coordinator. She began working with FBI on the booking, transportation, and accommodations across the country, along with working with I.R.S. to set up press as the tour went along. She did a great job. She was clear with the band that press was going to be important, and they had to dispel the rumors that they hated the press and that the press must beware of them. The group agreed, and the press was handled by Susan.

The group did a good job with the press, and even when they tried to take the piss out of some, they were at least good-natured about it, discussing things like UFOs, extraterrestrials, along with other strange and off-the-wall topics. A lot of interviews were set up prior to their arrival in various states and venues. The tour was set; first gig was in NYC.

The band arrived, we were all excited, and they received their itineraries, which also had information regarding any press they had to do and with whom. This was the first tour for Fast Forward Ltd., and it was set up in the right venues across the country. We got them a US tour manager given their UK one was not able to handle the tour. The STAGE was set.

The first gig was in a very good venue in the East Village called The Ritz, on 11th Street, between 3rd and 4th Avenues, in the East Village in NYC. It was built in 1886 and is a historic venue, originally called Webster Hall. In 1980, it became The Ritz. And, by 1992, it went back to its original name, Webster Hall. It's known for everything from being a union labor hall at the turn of the century, to the place for recording the likes of Frank Sinatra, Elvis, Dylan, and B.B. King. Even Bill Clinton held an event there.

The Ritz has an upstairs with tables around the balcony. No one's vision was blocked whether you stood downstairs or you sat upstairs. With a capacity of about 2500, it's still a great venue after all these years.

So, The Stranglers' first gig went off without a hitch. The show was a great one to start the tour. The band played their asses off. We had a good-sized audience, lots of excitement, and the crew was ready when the show was over to pack up and hit the road. We were off and running, or, better yet, touring!

THEN THE SHIT HIT THE FAN . . . but we made it work, ultimate TEAMWORK

Around 2 a.m., the two roadies who packed the gear in the truck, locked it up and went to a friend's place in the East Village to take a shower before getting on the road. To their surprise, when they were ready to leave, they found the truck was gone. Stolen! Everything was gone, except the guitars, which the musicians had with them in their hotel rooms. So now what? A lot of dealing with the police, a lot of driving around to see if the truck would show up some place, which it did weeks later, empty.

I went to the band and asked them if they wanted to continue the tour. I got a resounding YES. We brought in the crew and let them know the tour was going to continue. I then gave them some people to call to rent equipment in NYC. Given they had their itineraries, they could begin to call ahead to find needed gear with the help of the promoters. I got on the phone with I.R.S. Records to see if we could get some support. They said no, and I let the band know that if they were serious to continue, we, the management, Fast Forward Ltd., would finance the tour, and they could pay us back when they returned to the U.K.

All was good, and we began to find some gear in NYC. We did get some help from Ian Copeland, head of Frontier Booking, our tour agency. They began to call ahead also. Most of what was needed were keyboards and an amp or two. We were able to get much of the gear rented in NYC. However, we knew there would be times that Dave, the keyboard player, would have to improvise with what was available. So the tour began. Susan and I were on the phone daily with the crew, giving them updates on what gear was available for the coming shows along with any other helpful information they may have needed.

Once the tour got to Los Angeles, we flew out to meet them and lend a supporting hand. Everyone had done well, great teamwork, and were now in Los Angeles, some missing important gear was able to be rented, and life got a bit easier. My partner Marty came down from San Francisco and was so impressed with what the crew and band had done to get this far that he gave everyone on the crew $100 to go have fun, given we had a couple of days off before we worked our way up the coast to San Francisco. A small token of thanks for keeping the show on the road and it was well appreciated. The couple of days off also gave the band a chance to meet Marty for the first time.

First show in Los Angeles was at The Rainbow, a well-known venue where everyone from The Doors to Crosby, Stills, Nash & Young, to the Beach Boys had played on their way up. Most Los Angeles bands starting out with some notoriety played there.

One of the events that had become a big thing with the band was when they played their song "Nice and Sleazy." Various women would get on stage and dance to the song, along with sometimes stripping to nothing. This was popular in the UK, and word had spread to the United States. By now, of course, Hugh would invite anyone on to the stage to dance. Sometimes, it got a bit crowded. This was the only time during a set no one chased anyone off the stage, let them dance, let them take off their clothes, shake it all, and have a great time, which was had by all.

One of the strangest times for the "Nice and Sleazy" show was in San Francisco. Hugh asked if any of the women in the audience would like to come up and dance. By the way, the club was a good size, large audience, and it was located in an area where there are few adult clubs and adult bookstores. So, as people went up on stage during the song, lots of clothes came off. One especially was very noticeable. She was a six-foot woman who looked incredible. Once her clothes came off, it was obvious this person was a transsexual who still had his/her penis. The band was astonished, fell out laughing, and played along with her. She did the same thing for the second set and was invited back to the hotel where we all met her. JJ and Hugh had a grand old time having fun with her. One never knows who will get up, dance, and strip dance.

The tour continued up into Canada and across to Montreal and Toronto, then back to NYC. Both Susan and I stayed on the tour. If I remember, there was quite a bit of press being done from San Francisco across Canada, and Susan was kept quite busy. We also picked up a photographer, Ava. She was very nice, not in the way, and did a lot of photos. Some of her pictures are used here in this book. Since that tour, she's been living with Jet Black, the drummer, for more than 10 years. Thanks for the pictures, Ava!

The rented gear held up, and when we were back in NYC, the band played at a club uptown in the '70s called Privates, owned by Ashley Pandel. It was a very nice venue. Big upstairs with a large ballroom and good-sized stage, and then downstairs was a restaurant bar. This was where The Stranglers played first when we arrived back from the cross-country tour.

The night The Stranglers played, when the show was over, Diana Ross and Gene Simmons showed up backstage. Great meeting her, and, as for Gene, I had gone bowling with him in the Village before with Ian Grant and a publicist that Ian was using, so we at least knew each other a bit.

Then another show was offered at a venue called Bonds, in Times Square. The Clash had to move their date, and they offered a premium fee. This turned out to be a horrendous experience. First, they wanted the band to play at about 11 p.m. Okay. But then they pushed it back to after midnight, and then a money hassle came up. The band finally went on at about 1 a.m. to a half-filled hall. At least we were able to get the $10,000 agreed upon for the show, and we were paid prior to performing. The tour finally ended at least on a good note. The band and crew survived and flew home.

It was time to get more done, not only another album out in the States, but one also was due for EMI records in the UK. I.R.S. had put out *Stranglers IV*, so that was available, but they did very little publicity, and we were not very thrilled with them. We were able to make a deal with Stiff Records in the U.S., who were signing various punk artists to their label. They agreed to put out *The Gospel According to the Meninblack*, the most recent Stranglers' UK release. This was a concept album that dealt with religion, aliens, UFOs, and other off-the-wall stuff, a good fit for the Stiff label, who were a lot of good people and good fun to deal with.

BIG LESSON LEARNED: No matter what happens, if all parties involved with the project, the events, and the situation agree to keep going, make it happen, and keep their sanity intact, it will happen. This was a great example of teamwork. Yes, there was stress and anxiety, but we did it as a team, and the tour worked. Teamwork is at its best under duress.

HANGING OUT . . . and working in NYC

Living and working in NYC, the music industry had its own world. One got to know various club owners, restaurant owners, bar owners, etc. NYC being a 24-7 city that never sleeps, we found ourselves going out about midnight to some club or a place to eat and hang out. It was also during that time that cocaine was rampant wherever you went. You would see lines of people waiting to use the bathroom so they could go and snort up. It got so out of hand that, in some of the places, you would see people chopping out lines and snorting right at their tables. NYC got a bit wired, so to speak. The city that never sleeps sure got a new wakeup call, and it was a disaster for some. Many new addicts to cocaine were now part of the New York scene.

However, the city also gave us opportunity and some privileges, based upon who we were and being part of the entertainment industry. We had the so-called VIP pass to get into some of the best places for music, food, and just be able to hang out with friends. One place we enjoyed going to was TRAX. This place was uptown on the West side, off Broadway, in the '70s. It was located downstairs, below street level. It was large with a side room to be able to have a drink, snack, and as usual, hang out. The larger room had a good-sized stage where anyone could get up and play (only if they were good). At any given night, you could see and hear a jam session from not only some of the best New York musicians, but also some of the well-known folks who were on tour and now had time to relax and enjoy.

One of the acts that played a lot there and would have various artists sit in was John Belushi and Dan Aykroyd's Blues Brothers, and they were great live! I don't remember if this was a place that they liked to rehearse or just hang, but they were there a lot. I ran into people from Led Zeppelin, the Rolling Stones, and more. I just don't remember them all, but this was a fun place to hear live music and spend some time.

Susan and I still hung out at Home, given we were pinball-machine players and they had a great machine to use. Also, we often went to a very nice restaurant on 12th Street, between 5th and 6th Avenues. We'd meet up with friends, drink wine, snack, and do our normal hanging out stuff. The place was called Christie's. This was where we spent time with friends outside of the music world. Another nice place was Ashley's, a dance club/restaurant on 5th Avenue and 13th Street, downtown, owned by Ashley Pandel. Ashley's had a restaurant downstairs with a disco upstairs. Both Susan and I also spent a good deal of time there also. It was an easy place to eat, meet people, and have some fun. Quite a few celebrities also spent time there. I remember Susan and I spending time with a couple of the members of The Kinks; I also remember running into John Lennon and Harry Neilson, along with other folks who came to eat and just relax and enjoy a place that was not wall-to-wall people, at least not in the restaurant area. One instance that I remember on an off night was going to the bathroom and running into John Belushi and O. J. Simpson. I said my hellos and then proceeded to ask O.J. what O.J. stood for. Belushi quickly answered "Orthodox Jew." So now I knew and I left with a big smile. One never knows who you could run into and where in NYC.

A lot of music business seemed to get done or at least get talked about while we were out at these various places. You could always count on running into someone from the industry. If there was good music playing, it was a given. Even if you were not involved in the music industry during the late '70s and early '80s, NYC was the place to party and hang out, whether that was good or bad.

As I mentioned before, The Ritz was a great place to hear good acts and do some business. One could sit and talk at tables and still see and hear the acts perform. Another good place was the Irving Plaza, which I believe is now called The Fillmore, after Bill Graham's Fillmore East on 2nd Avenue. They, too, booked good acts from all over the world that were on their way up the popular ladder.

BACK TO ROCK AND ROLL . . .
back to work, we hung out enough

I found myself flying back and forth from the UK. Jerome Brailey was not doing very much. He was having trouble getting it together to tour and promote his second album. There was nothing I could do. He needed to get on tour. I had the agents ready to book him. Columbia Records was going to do some promotion, but I was getting busier. The Stranglers were doing a lot of UK touring and some in Europe, promoting *The Raven* and *The Gospel According to the Meninblack*. Most of the time in the UK, I was with the band, EMI records, working on promotion, or with John Giddings who was planning the next tour. I also would meet with the band's lawyers and accountants, making sure things were going smoothly. I began to feel pressure from the band to move to the UK, but I was not ready yet nor was it on my radar screen.

I remember one particular flight over to the U.K.; I was going to spend a week working on getting the band a new publishing deal. Their present one was ending, and I knew the challenge was how much I could get and what kind of deal for the administration of their publishing was going to be offered. I wanted to go for a $200,000 deal and only 15 percent to the publisher for admin work. Before I left for London, I had made various appointments with a lot of record companies/publishing companies, such as Columbia, Virgin, EMI (this one would be for renewal of the present deal), and various others. Every day, I had a meeting.

My most memorable one was with Virgin. I met with Richard Branson (one of my present business idols). We had a good conversation, but no deal. He did send me off to my next appointment in one of his limos. He definitely is a class act. I had gotten nowhere after four days.

When I got back to the hotel, I was told that there was someone waiting for me in the hotel restaurant. I was tired, worn out, and a bit depressed that I had not closed a deal. Sitting in the restaurant, I saw the head of publishing for EMI. We had not yet met. He was too busy to set a meeting, but there he was. I sat down, and we began to talk. I told him what I was looking for. He didn't blink an eye. He said he would get back to me the next day prior to my flight home. EMI had the band's publishing over the years and knew what it could mean in revenue for them, especially with compilation albums of past hits. We shook hands, and I said, "Hear from you tomorrow." I ate and went to bed.

The next day, early in the morning, I got a call and I was told we got the deal we wanted. I got hold of the band, their lawyers, and accountants and got the ball moving right away. By the following week, the deal was signed with EMI, and we all smiled. It was a very good deal, and lots of people were surprised we only had to give up 15 percent for administration.

On another trip to the UK, I got a call from Susan, who woke me up to tell me that John Lennon had been shot and was killed. I was in shock and that day, I had to go to EMI, which was not a good place given the Beatles were involved with the label. It was a very sad day in London, around the world, and EMI was full of tears, as was I. Given I had spent time with his backup band and respected John to no end, how could someone do this? It was the talk no matter where I went or who I saw; there was a conversation about John and the sadness we all felt. The entire UK was in mourning. It was in the air and rightly so.

There was now talk about a new album by The Stranglers. EMI wanted a bigger seller than they had with *The Raven* and *The Gospel*. This was understood, given they just signed a new publishing deal, and the band was on the right track with the press along with the songs they were writing. The band disliked producers and wanted to do it themselves. However, EMI was pushing for Tony Visconti to produce and get some of the songs sounding more commercial. Tony had worked with the likes of David Bowie and had a long track record of hits. So he was brought in.

While the album was being worked on, Susan and I got married and decided to move to London. Things were getting very busy, and it was better being there than flying back and forth every couple of weeks. So a week after we got married, we were looking for a flat to live in London. What was supposed to be set up for us fell through. We found ourselves in London, looking for a hotel to at least get settled enough to find a place to live.

We did get two weeks at a beautiful townhouse in the SOHO section of London. It had a bit of a story. We were told someone was murdered there. Strange, but we needed a base to begin looking for a flat. We didn't experience any ghosts or weird noises in the middle of the night (ha-ha), so we were fine. Finally, we did find a one-bedroom flat in an area called Mornington Crescent, at the foot of Camden Town, an area of London close to where we needed to be. We now had easy access to EMI, the group, and various agents, lawyers, and accountants. Off we went to work. New shows were booked, and recording was going well.

LESSON LEARNED: Have everything set up and do it yourself prior to moving to the UK or any place else. You would think we would have known better, given our experience setting up and running tours. No excuses.

One funny story took place when the band was playing at the Rainbow Theatre in London. Susan and I had arrived at the stage door and were stopped by some guy dressed nicely who said we could not come in. I asked why. He said he was the band's manager and was not letting anyone in he didn't know. That lasted about 30 seconds. I got a hold of one of our security guards, and this guy was removed gently. Back to the new album.

Tony Visconti was doing a great job, given we were not hearing any complaints from the group. They had their artistic control, but with Tony involved, he was able to keep the tracks under control. The end result was the release of the album, *La Folie*.

We got EMI to do good promotion, but the first single, "Let Me Introduce You to the Family," only charted at #42. The next single, "Golden Brown," went to #2 on the singles chart, and the album went to #11. To this day, "Golden Brown" remains their biggest hit.

The album's success now brought back the conversation about returning to the United States, doing a tour, and promoting *La Folie* along with "Golden Brown."

I knew what they wanted of EMI, and their record deal was ready to be negotiated. I had also come up with what I thought was a very good deal for the US. Sire Records wanted to release *La Folie* in the US, promote it, give the band $50,000 in tour support with no payback, and it was offered only as a one-album deal. EMI was going to let them go if they wanted, but wanted one more album as well. This, too, was a great deal. They were going to get what they wanted, out of EMI, a US release with good promotion, and tour support. Sire Records was the perfect label for them. Sire had the Pretenders, The Ramones, Talking Heads, and Echo and the Bunnymen, along with many others. They knew how to promote punk, new wave, and underground artists.

A one-album deal like what was being offered was amazing. So I sat down with the group once I had all the pieces in place. They knew I was working on this along with a new European label deal. We discussed the positive points of it all. They had nothing to lose. One new tour of the States, which with the tour support would be great, and one more album with EMI. This would leave the time to really look for a new multi-album deal. So we discussed and discussed these issues every time we could.

The band members had a pact among themselves. Either they would all agree, or they would do nothing. JJ and Hugh said yes, but Jet and Dave said no. And no matter who spoke with them—their lawyers, their agents, or their accountants—they were unmovable. They felt they didn't need the United States. They were generating a lot of money via tours, with their latest hit album *La Folie* along with past albums. They already had a good publishing deal; what more did they want or need? I began to have side meetings with JJ and Hugh to see if they could push the other two. They understood the possibilities of becoming more world-renowned. If the album sold well in the United States, it would raise the ante to get the band a new label deal, and they would be worth a lot more.

We hit a stone wall. Jet and Dave were not going to move. So what were we doing in the UK? Our relationship with The Stranglers was coming to an end. Susan disliked living in London. I'm sure if we stayed, we would have picked up another group or two. We did gain some very strong credibility, having managed The Stranglers and bringing in their biggest hit.

Susan missed NYC terribly and wanted to go home, and I was not going to put up a big battle and lose my wife of one year. We knew we had gotten them very good lawyers and accountants. John Giddings would keep them working, and they could deal with EMI as they saw fit, which by the way they did. They left EMI and went to EPIC. No big event or big album and, as time went on, they jumped to other labels with no great results. JJ once told me they had sold 24 million albums, so money was not a problem. Okay, but what I saw was somewhat similar to what I saw back with Everyone. I call this FEAR OF SUCCESS. Two of them wanted to go and take up the challenge and the adventure. There was nothing in their way. But they didn't take the chance. We split up.

It is amazing how people make it to a level and don't keep going. They get comfortable, things get easier, and they don't see any future possibilities. So The Stranglers keep playing in the UK along with some European dates, still put out CDs, and have no big hits since *La Folie,* and still hopefully enjoy their life, not thinking of what it may have become had they taken the chance. Hugh Cornwell left the band for a solo career not long after I was gone. He still is touring and still putting out CDs. I hear from Hugh when he comes to the States, and I'm in contact with Ava (the photographer from Canada), Jet's girlfriend, on Facebook, and we communicate at times. In fact, she has set me up with a person who is writing a book called *Peaches* about The Stranglers. The title is the name of one of the group's early hits, and he wanted to interview me (which he did) regarding some of the stuff I experienced with the band while I was their tour manager and then their manager.

Thanks to my connection with Ava, I'm still in tune with the new stuff The Stranglers are doing. It all can't be bad. In fact, it may have worked out for them. So who knows, maybe they were right to do it their way. It just wasn't mine. I wanted to shoot for the moon and beyond.

One of the interesting things about being in the UK was meeting some really fascinating people and spending a bit of time with them. I remember being with Paul McGuinness, the manager of U2, and having coffee and drinks with him and Bono at the Portobello Hotel. We also spent time when Paul came to the United States, and we hung out some.

There were various groups that I had met, too many to mention. I used to play backgammon with the person who was handling The Eurythmics prior to them becoming famous. I had a chance to possibly manage them, given at the time we had a hit single and a hit album on our hands with The Stranglers, but Susan and I were talking about moving back to the United States. So we didn't pursue this, and we had no idea how good they were. Sometimes, we all pass on the unknown for the known, which was keeping my marriage together.

We also met Bob Hoskins, the actor. He was a friend of Hugh Cornwell, and we went to see him in a very good Sam Shepard play called *True West*. We went backstage after the performance, and he gave us a ride back to our flat. Later on, after returning to NYC, Bob gave us a call when he was in town. We took him to dinner, to a great place called the Buffalo Roadhouse (too bad it's gone) and got him to eat the best burger he had ever had. Nice guy. We never got to meet up again, but that was something that happens in the industry. Everyone is busy with their career, and it is hit and miss to see people again that you hit it off with. Bob is a great actor and went on to do some fabulous movies. People come and go, but those that you get to spend a bit of time with are great, and the talk is not all about one's career—more just about what is going on, what is important to each of us, and, of course, some business opportunities that we may be experiencing. But you leave the ego at the door.

Too many people to even begin to mention, but it was fun for this Jersey City kid who, as you know, could roll a joint, and living in the UK, I was able to show them what I did years ago with Ginger Baker of Cream. Thin joints get you just as high, if not better. At least there's no tobacco in your lungs. More **Joint Ventures**, I type with a smile!

LESSONS LEARNED: No matter what business you're in, be careful of your choices, think them through, and get advice if you're stuck. Think where you want to go with your career. We all can make mistakes, but we have to learn from them and move on and not make the same ones again.

BACK HOME . . . and what comes next

Susan and I moved back to the States, to our West Village apartment to regroup and move on. Time was 1982. I began to look for new artists to manage and spread the word to various agents, accountants, and lawyers that I knew. I picked up John Cale, one of the founding members of Velvet Underground. He lived just up the street from me in the West Village, along with his wife. We got along well, and I helped him sort out his record deal with Z Records and get that on go. He had an agent, and he was being booked as a solo artist.

Nice guy, but he had a woman stalking him, and this was beginning to get serious. She claimed to be his wife when we finally got her into court. Of course, the case was thrown out. He was given a restraining order against her, which didn't work all that well. She used to ring his doorbell in the middle of the night and then he would call me and at times I called the police. Finally, it calmed down.

I also still had Jerome Brailey, with whom we just seemed to part ways. I had left for a year in the UK and nothing was going on with him as far as I remember. These days, I see him on Facebook and we have contacted each other recently. He has his own label and I wish him all the success one can have. He is still making music and doing some shows. He is a good guy and a great drummer.

I was introduced to an up-and-coming publicist soon after I got back from the UK. She was able to get an interview done with me and printed in the commentary section of *Billboard* magazine. This was great because it got my name out there, and I was able to mention various UK acts that no one in the States had yet heard of. We found that the UK and Europe were a bit more progressive in what they played on the radio. We found UK radio to be very interesting and very enlightening. The *Billboard* article generated a few interviews with various artists. Some which were real assholes during the interview, and I passed on them. As far as I know, none of them ever made it. I did a little representation in the United States for Big Country and The Members, two UK acts managed by Ian Grant, who was one of the co-managers of The Stranglers when I was their tour manager. He is a good guy, and we had stayed in touch after I left the UK. He had started Cairo management and had a pretty big hit with Big Country, and it was my pleasure to help him out when he asked. Glad we still stay in touch once in a while these days.

LESSON LEARNED: I am glad that I walked away from some of these acts. They very well could have cost me a ton of money, and most likely would have been a pain in the ass. Sometimes, in business, one has to walk away from a potential client due to it not being a good fit. It should never be just about the money. It has to be a good fit with respect, confidence, and you, as a manager, have to be their trusted adviser.

Commentary

Playing It Safe—And Dull

By ED KLEINMAN

When WABC recently changed formats, the newspapers headlined "The Day The Music Died." Considering the music that WABC and other American radio stations are currently playing, or more accurately not playing, this headline could become much more widespread in the months ahead.

Having spent the last 12 months in England, I was amazed by the difference between the music programmed for listeners here and overseas. At this moment, the music available via the BBC and Capitol services in England is interesting and adventurous. By comparison, most American radio seems safe and boring.

It is this lack of variety that is turning listeners and record buyers away. Looking for alternative music, the consumer has deserted his familiar radio station and local record store. The amazing growth of "Walkman" units does not bode well for broadcasters or record retailers.

The record companies are no less to blame. In recent years they have played it so safe that they have all but neglected the backbone of the record industry—the young record buyer.

Kleinman: "Successful musical changes have always come from new people trying new things."

Faced with figures showing that the Woodstock generation is now well into its 30s, the record companies have designed their release schedules to appeal to this now older taste. As a result, we get the same records recycled over and over.

The names that made musical history are still releasing records, although few of them have anything new to say.

highly successful English groups that are currently making inroads in this country.

A group like Orchestral Manoeuver may not be commercial by American standards but is highly creative musically, and able to achieve passable sales in the English marketplace. Surely there should be some place besides college radio where music like this can be heard.

Soft Cell, the Human League, the Witnesses, and the Blasters are other groups who have had some measure of success here and exemplify the music so sorely missing on today's radio.

Handling the affairs of a group that isn't Top 10 is a 24-hour-a-day job, and means getting the group 100% involved. Managing is helping a group reach its full potential.

When record companies and radio stations are non-supportive, creative management, such as practiced through the years by the Bill Grahams, Herbie Herberts and Miles Copelands, goes a long way toward keeping a group moving in a positive direction. Not every group can go all the way, but without this effort and support they have no chance.

Companies like Stiff America and IRS Records should be complimented for remembering that tomorrow's musical fad is today's avant garde.

Not too many years ago the Ramones and Talking Heads were considered unplayable by the radio honchos. A great deal

'The names that made musical history are still releasing records, although few of them have anything new to say'

The current emphasis by the legends of rock'n'roll on updated, albeit less inventive versions of their old ideas ignores the fact that all musical revolutions, from the Charleston to big band swing to Elvis Presley to the Beatles or Rolling Stones, originated with a younger, less blasé buying element.

It is this audience that is being ignored both by today's radio stations and record companies.

Successful musical changes have always come from new people trying new things. So-called "New Wave" music could not possibly take hold with the mass audience until it has been discovered, promoted and refined by younger musical tastes.

The lawyers and accountants, who run most of today's record companies, tend to go along with the tide. It's the easy way, but not necessarily the most profitable in the long run.

Independent labels in England seem to not only survive, but to flourish. Haircut 100, XTC, Jam and Bow-Wow-Wow are all

of hard work and a positive response from audiences forced radio to reverse its stand.

There are no absolutes when it comes to programming, but too often minds and ears are closed to anything different.

It's time our more adventurous broadcasters take a look at some new musical possibilities. Maybe it means programming new music once an hour, once a day, once a week or some other formula. The MTV experience and a similar experience with HBO's "Video Jukebox" seems to prove that there is a big audience out there waiting eagerly to hear something new and different.

One thing is sure. If they don't find it in local radio, we will be seeing more headlines in more cities about "The Day The Music Died."

Ed Kleinman is president of Fast Forward Ltd., currently representing Cairo Management in the U.S. He is the former manager of the Stranglers.

From *Billboard* magazine, June 1982.

Other things were going on, however. Susan had enough of the music business and wanted to go to law school. She began studying for the LSATs. My mom was dying of pancreatic cancer and was in a hospital a few blocks away from where we lived in NYC. I visited her almost every day. We had money in the bank, we had quarterly publishing revenues coming in from The Stranglers, but I was not giving 100+ percent of me to my artists or even spending the right amount of time with finding new clients. So now what?

CHANGES . . . again and more

Things got slow. I was still dealing with personal stuff. Marty came East, and we sat down and discussed everything from where were some of the people we knew in the business that were like us and to where had they disappeared. We didn't owe anyone any money. The Stranglers' publishing royalties were still coming in, which we eventually sold back to them after two years.

After a few drinks, we decided it was time to shut down the business and take the money and run, so to speak. By then, John Cale was our only client. We would find him a new manager, one that he would be comfortable with, and we would shake hands, say good-bye, good luck, much success, and take no future royalties.

Marty got his money, I got some, and off we went. This, of course, took some time, but when done, we were over. We had our run.

Susan did well on her LSATs and was applying for law schools. My mom had passed away, and our NYC apartment was going condo/ coop, and we didn't have the money to buy it, especially if Susan was going to law school. The best I could do was go work for my brother at his technical trade school business outside Philadelphia. This was not great for Susan since she didn't want to leave NYC, but she did get accepted to Temple Law School and graduated in 1986.

So there for a JOINT, I spent 18 years in and around the music industry. I met many people over that time, from stars, up-and-coming stars, would-be stars that never got shining. I met business people who still are in the industry, along with people who worked as I did, some of whom I'm still in contact with. I met good people who were helpful, people who wanted a free ride, and a share of assholes that hang around the business, hoping for who knows what. Too many to remember all of them, and at 68 years old, I smile and I am glad I remembered this much.

Not sure my timeline is totally accurate, but I'm sure it's close enough for ROCK AND ROLL. It was a great experience, and even today, if I had what I think would be about a half million dollars to invest knowing that it all could be a lost investment, I would do it again. Based upon how much I now know about the business world, marketing, and sales, this would be a great challenge that I would enjoy to no end.

The final set was played. The Joint was out. The curtain came down, and the lights were dimmed. I still can hear the music and the applause at times in my head, but . . . NO ENCORE.

Rhinoceros
1968

Genya Ravan, former lead singer of Ten Wheel Drive
2013

Pig Iron
1970

Elephant's Memory
1972

John Lennon and May Pang
1973

May Pang
2013

May Pang and Ed Kleinman
2012

Everyone
1975

Everyone
1976

Jerome Brailey, formerly of Jerome Brailey & Mutiny
and former drummer for Parliament-Funkadelic
1980

Jerome Brailey
2013

The Stranglers

Ed Kleinman and Susan Erlichman, of Fast Forward Ltd.
1981

The Stranglers' security team

A "Nice and Sleazy" dancer from The Stranglers' 1980 tour

Jet Black, of The Stranglers
circa 1980

JJ Burnel, of The Stranglers
circa 1980

Dave Greenfield, of The Stranglers
circa 1980

Hugh Cornwell, of The Stranglers
circa 1980

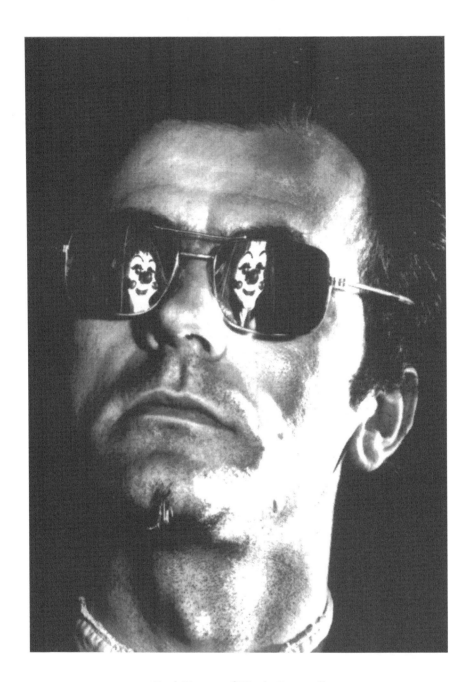

Cool Picture of Hugh Cornwell

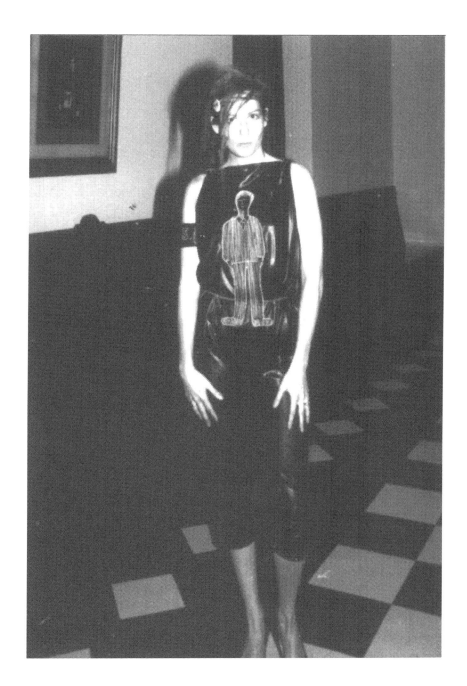

Ava, photographer for The Stranglers
circa 1980

TRANSITION . . . into sales, leadership, and beyond

We moved to the Philly area. I went to work for my brother as a sales coordinator for his 10 sales people, all very experienced. My salvation was that I was the owner's brother. I got hassled by some of the top sales people, especially since, as one said, "You've not been on the street, what do you know? Get a kit, go sell, go prove yourself."

This sounded like some rock-and-roll headaches. Been there, done that with egos.

So I got a kit, which was a three-ring binder to use for show-and-tell on a sales call. However, I knew that if I asked the right questions, especially, "Why do you want to go into computer repair?" I might get the potential student to buy and not have me to hard sell.

If you perform well, people listen and may buy. I had to perform, but the prospect had to buy. In 1985, computer repair was an up-and-coming industry, and we had more than 1000 students in the school. So finding prospects was not the issue. Closing was.

Well, I used what I knew from the music world. It was the experience that I had, and at the end of the month, I had closed one less than the top sales person. I put the kit on my brother's desk and said, "That is enough of the out-on-the-street sales."

I had gained a lot of credibility with the salespeople, and I became their sales manager. Yes, I needed more experience, but on issues I couldn't handle due to lack of knowledge or experience in that area, I could call on my brother, and he would handle it. I must have done well, given three years later, I was asked to go to Maryland and take over the sales department (admissions) for three schools he bought there. Off I went.

Susan graduated law school in 1986 and got a position at a law firm in Philly, and we split up for a while. I began running the sales in all three schools in the Baltimore area, and when the school was sold, I moved on to other technical schools.

Susan and I had reconciled and, by 1988, we were living together in Baltimore. In 1993, our son Michael was born. Susan returned to work three months later. The company I was working for had closed and I stayed home for almost a year with our son. I did what I called a John Lennon, staying home with Michael as he did with his son Sean.

When the time came, I found a position as a sales coach for the firm Sandler Sales Institute, which sold franchises in sales and sales management training. I had no idea what a sales coach did, but I learned what executive coaching was all about from David Sandler, the owner/developer of the company. Good way to learn. I spent six-and-a-half years with them, then moved on as an independent contractor for The Objective Management Group and learned how to be even better as an executive business coach in the sales force development arena. I stayed with them for more than 13 years.

Today, I have my own company doing executive business development coaching, and I thank all those I met, learned from, and became colleagues and friends with.

EPILOGUE, IT'S ONLY ROCK AND ROLL AND I LIKE IT, LIKE IT, LIKE IT . . . lessons learned, lessons used from the music world into the executive coaching world, today, tomorrow, and beyond

What I learned in the music business over 18 years has helped me in my sales force development role over the past 20 years (time flies when you're having fun). I hope I'm still learning, still rockin', still helping those in business, and still helping others where I can.

Starting out in the music world, it didn't matter what level I was on; there was always something to learn, and it was fun. I'm not sure I took it seriously for quite a while. It was just a way to earn a bit of money, travel, and have fun. Remember, "I'm with the band."

In the early days, it was about setting the stage, dealing with equipment, and working with people on and off the stage. As I went from roadie to tour manager, I began to realize some of the things I had learned so far and the importance of those lessons. I learned how important relationship building was and still is. Once I was a manager of my own business and had my own clients, it became evident how important it was to have connections and gain respect and trust, not only from your clients, but also from the people you have to deal with. I carried this over into the sales arena, from sales training, sales force development, and on to executive coaching.

The show must go on and go on in a way that your fans, your clients, buy what you're selling. Buy because they want to, not because you're pushing it down their throats. They buy because of their enjoyment of your music or, in other types of business, their need for your product, service, or expertise.

It doesn't matter if you are a musician and you are performing, whether it is in a small bar or an arena with thousands in attendance, you want to sell your music, sell your performance, so you are booked again, so that you can get more fans, more concerts, and grow your audience. You have to perform at the top of your game. If not, you won't gain more fans. In fact, you will lose them. You won't sell CDs, downloads, t-shirts, or get rebooked and grow into stardom, if that is your dream, your desire.

You are selling YOU and what you have to offer. You are the product. It's your music, your stage presence, and your belief in your product, and your audience, as I said, your fans or clients buy you as a whole package.

It's the same in any business. If you have a product or service to sell, you are still on stage. You have something that the clients or prospects may need to help their companies grow, stay effective, and function in the marketplace. Bottom line is to generate profitable revenues and gain consistent growth. Your clients may not know what they need unless it's a broken piece or lack of something they feel they want. No matter what, you have to perform. They have to discover you can help. They have to trust you and believe you have what it takes. Don't forget, they're buying you.

If you don't perform, they will go to your competition. Or, if they do hire you or buy your product and you or your product fails, you get fired or at least they don't hire you again in the future. When they're playing golf with other business owners and your name comes up, they let folks know that you have a shitty album, so to speak. You performed like you didn't know what you were doing, and they tell their friends not to hire you. They feel they were sold something that didn't work.

Well, that happened in the music world also. The show was a waste of time, poor sound, poor performance, and you bought the music based on one song and found out that was all they had. You spent good money and got no results. I can't stress the importance of performing to perfection, and it does take time to get there. Remember, don't make the same mistake twice.

When you are in the entertainment world, you need an audience who wants to see you again and again and who enjoys what you have to sell. If you are in sales of any type, the client/prospect wants results from what they buy. You both have egos, you both want more fans/ clients, and you both want people to refer you to their friends and colleagues. You both want more notoriety, more business, and you both want to be stars in your world. Poor performance then leads to no sales, no new clients, no renewal of your record deal or product or service, no new tours, no referrals to friends, and no word on the street that one should buy your product or service. YOU ARE OUT Of BUSINESS.

You both have to be held accountable even if all you can do is hold yourself accountable. Both of you want to be stars, and to be such, you must keep learning, keep getting better, and keep getting positive results. Remember, it's all rock and roll. Whether you are selling growth, products, or entertainment, you must stay on top of your game.

After all the years in the industry and all the musicians I had met and was involved with, one would think that I would have learned how to play an instrument. At least the guitar. But I'd like to think that I was more into the business side than the playing side. Even so, I am just plain lazy when it comes to practicing the guitar.

However, I do continue to learn and practice my executive coaching consistently. I know what a poor performance is. One must practice one's chosen craft. Practice does not necessarily make perfect, but practice can make you better.

As for the guitar, maybe I will get it right in the future. I've been taking lessons for the past two years. I now can at least jam with my teacher on some stuff and I really enjoy the hour per week we spend together. Goal: to play a blues song at my seventieth birthday a few years from now. Mmm, I better get a bit more serious. Time is running out.

FINAL LESSON LEARNED: Keep **THE JOINT VENTURES** for your days off. Those who are successful are always learning no matter what arena you are performing in. Believe in yourself, always have goals. It's not about you, it's about your fans or clients. Be the best you can and, I can't say it enough, perform at your maximum all the time, practice and learn and most of all . . .

KEEP ROCKIN'

Made in the USA
San Bernardino, CA
20 December 2015